# Amphibians and Reptiles of the Carolinas and Virginia

Bernard S. Martof

William M. Palmer

Joseph R. Bailey

Julian R. Harrison III

Photographs by

Jack Dermid

# Amphibians and Reptiles of the Carolinas and Virginia

The University of North Carolina Press  Chapel Hill

© 1980 The University of North Carolina Press
Photographs © 1980 Jack Dermid
All rights reserved
Manufactured in the United States of America
04  03  02  01  00    9  8  7  6  5
Library of Congress Cataloging in Publication Data
Main entry under title:

Amphibians and reptiles of the Carolinas and Virginia.

  Bibliography: p.
  Includes index.
  1. Amphibians—North Carolina—Identification.
2. Amphibians—South Carolina—Identification.
3. Amphibians—Virginia—Identification. 4. Reptiles
—North Carolina—Identification. 5. Reptiles—South
Carolina—Identification. 6. Reptiles—Virginia—
Identification. I. Martof, Bernard Stephen, 1920–78
QL653.N8A4    597.9'0975  79-11790
ISBN 0-8078-1389-3
ISBN 0-8078-4252-4

*The University of North Carolina Press is grateful to
the family of the late Helen Thornton Brooks of Greensboro,
North Carolina, for its generous support of the publication
of this book.*

*This book is dedicated to
the memory of Bernard S. Martof,
our friend and coauthor,
whose untimely death, just as
the manuscript was completed,
has left a melancholy void in the
herpetology of the Carolinas
and Virginia*

# Contents

# Amphibians and Reptiles of the Carolinas and Virginia

# Introduction

Amphibians and reptiles are important in nature and many are highly beneficial to man. They have long had great appeal to the amateur naturalist, as well as the professional zoologist. In the past few decades, information about these fascinating animals has grown markedly. Furthermore, the explosive spread of suburban living and outdoor recreation has evoked a resurgence of interest in the identification, natural history, behavior, and distribution of organisms, especially amphibians and reptiles. Many species also do well in captivity and make amusing pets. This book was written to acquaint persons with the abundant and varied herpetofauna of Virginia and the Carolinas and to encourage the growth of knowledge about, and understanding of, these organisms. We hope this book will be useful to herpetologists, other biologists, naturalists, and indeed all persons concerned about the environment and the quality of life.

Virginia and North and South Carolina, three broadly contiguous states, constitute a compact natural area bordered by the mountains to the northwest, the Atlantic Ocean to the northeast and southeast, and the Savannah River to the southwest. The three states harbor 159 species of amphibians and reptiles. About a third are wide-ranging species shared by all three states: 26 species occur areawide and 28 others inhabit two-thirds or more of the area. Furthermore, the area contains 4 endemic species and 14 others nearly restricted to it, thus providing numerous unique elements (see Table I).

A species includes a population or a group of populations whose members share many traits and are readily distinguishable from individuals of other species. They interbreed or are capable of interbreeding but are reproductively isolated from individuals of other species. Some species are subdivided into races, or subspecies. Such populations are morphologically or physiologically distinct and inhabit only a part of the geographic range of the species. Only a few of the more conspicuous subspecies are mentioned in this publication.

The species here included are those generally recognized by most herpetologists; however, for questionable or controversial species, our choices of the alternatives (often not unanimous) are

**Table I** Faunal Composition

| ORDER | FAMILIES | GENERA | | | |
|---|---|---|---|---|---|
| Suborder | | | Total | Endemic | Nearly Endemic |
| Caudata | 7 | 16 | 52 | 4 | 11 |
| Salientia | 5 | 8 | 31 | 0 | 3 |
| Crocodilia | 1 | 1 | 1 | 0 | 0 |
| Chelonia | 7 | 16 | 24 | 0 | 0 |
| Squamata Sauria | 4 | 7 | 12 | 0 | 0 |
| Serpentes | 3 | 23 | 39 | 0 | 0 |
| Total | 27 | 71 | 159 | 4 | 14 |

**SPECIES**

| Areawide | Mountains | Piedmont | Coastal Plain | VA | NC | SC |
|---|---|---|---|---|---|---|
| 5 | 39 | 23 | 24 | 39 | 42 | 32 |
| 4 | 14 | 19 | 29 | 24 | 29 | 30 |
| 0 | 0 | 0 | 1 | 0 | 1 | 1 |
| 3 | 11 | 13 | 19 | 22 | 19 | 19 |
| 3 | 9 | 9 | 11 | 8 | 10 | 12 |
| 11 | 23 | 31 | 37 | 30 | 37 | 38 |
| 26 | 96 | 95 | 121 | 123 | 138 | 132 |

used. Divergence of opinion arises mainly because species evolve and also because knowledge of many populations is so fragmentary. Many species are capable of becoming divided into geographically isolated populations, each of which may accumulate genetic differences and become morphologically or physiologically distinct. If such a population remains geographically isolated, its taxonomic status (whether it is an unusually distinct subspecies or a full-fledged species) is often a subjective judgment. However, if the two populations in question become sympatric, their taxonomic status is often easily ascertained. If, in the zone of overlap, the parental phenotypes occur frequently and hybrids only occasionally, taxonomists conclude that barriers to interbreeding exist and that the populations are separate species. On the other hand, if most individuals in the central part of the zone of overlap have some of the diagnostic features of both parental forms, then the populations are best classed as conspecific. The problem of recognizing species is further exacerbated because some populations become reproductively isolated (do not interbreed) but are phenotypically similar or identical (sibling or cryptic species).

In spite of numerous attempts to standardize the common names of amphibians and reptiles, much remains to be done. An obstacle to standardization, of course, is that different names for a species are deeply entrenched in various regions of the country. In general, our common names follow those recommended in 1978 by the Society for the Study of Amphibians and Reptiles, but we have departed in a few cases where we believe our selections more appropriately describe the animal. For example, the three local species of *Necturus* are called Mudpuppies, and *N. lewisi* is the Carolina Mudpuppy rather than the Neuse River Waterdog since it also occurs in the Tar River system and is endemic to North Carolina. Our other choices are Cherokee rather than Seepage Salamander for *Desmognathus aeneus*, Cumberland rather than Black Mountain Salamander for *Desmognathus welteri*, Cow Knob rather than White-spotted Salamander for *Plethodon punctatus*, Eastern Musk Turtle rather than Stinkpot for *Sternotherus odoratus*, and Carolina rather than Green Anole for *Anolis carolinensis*.

All species but one are native to the area; the sole exception is the Texas Horned Lizard. Although several other species have been introduced, none shows signs of establishing breeding colonies. On the other hand, some exotic populations of species native to our area have been introduced, e.g., the Red-eared Slider (a subspecies of the Yellowbelly Slider, *Chrysemys scripta*) is well established in some large ponds in Durham and Wake counties, North Carolina, and probably elsewhere. There is also evidence of intra-area and extraarea transport of native animals, chiefly resulting from the use of amphibians as fish bait and reptiles as pets. More impressive changes in distribution are associated with agriculture, dam building, mining, coastal alterations, burgeoning suburban development, and highway construction. No extinctions of our herpetofauna are known to have occurred in historical times. We wish to keep it that way! On the other hand, numerous deletions have occurred in many parts of the area, and turbulent times lie ahead.

Recognizing that man has drastically altered habitats and eliminated many species, Congress passed the Endangered Species Act in 1973. There are several compelling reasons why we must prevent the extinction of species: (1) We share with other organisms a common evolutionary heritage, and we find kinship, inspiration, and beauty in many of them. (2) Human populations are large, complexly interrelated, and vulnerable to extinction. We have much to gain from studies of other imperiled populations. (3) More practically, as genetic and biochemical resources other organisms are indispensable in biological and medical research. Clearly, the most effective protection of endangered species is that provided by preservation of the natural habitats. Not only do we need more large parks and wilderness areas, but many communities would benefit immeasurably by having their own programs of habitat preservation.

To promote interest in our diminishing herpetofauna, we have listed those species requiring special protection in Table II, which is based mainly on special conferences recently held in each state. Three levels of vulnerability to extinction are indicated: endangered —those in imminent danger, threatened—those with reduced populations in a large portion of their ranges, and concern—those which may disappear from our area or those about which only scant information is available. Even though federal and state laws impose heavy penalties for the possession or sale of several of these species, all need the maximum protection we can provide.

Inasmuch as this book may inspire its readers into new and inquisitive channels, a few words about conserving, collecting, and keeping amphibians and reptiles are provided. No longer can the woods, fields, lakes, and streams and their inhabitants be ex-

**Table II** Imperiled Species

| | | SC | NC | VA |
|---|---|---|---|---|
| *Cryptobranchus alleganiensis* | Hellbender | C | C | C |
| *Siren lacertina* | Greater Siren | – | C | C |
| *Pseudobranchus striatus* | Dwarf Siren | C | | |
| *Necturus lewisi* | Carolina Mudpuppy | | C | |
| *Necturus maculosus* | Common Mudpuppy | | C | C |
| *Ambystoma cingulatum* | Flatwoods Salamander | C | | |
| *Ambystoma talpoideum* | Mole Salamander | – | C | |
| *Ambystoma tigrinum* | Tiger Salamander | C | C | C |
| *Desmognathus wrighti* | Pigmy Salamander | | – | C |
| *Leurognathus marmoratus* | Shovelnose Salamander | – | – | C |
| *Eurycea junaluska* | Junaluska Salamander | | C | |
| *Plethodon dorsalis* | Zigzag Salamander | | C | |
| *Plethodon hubrichti* | Peaks of Otter Salamander | | | C |
| *Plethodon punctatus* | Cow Knob Salamander | | | C |
| *Plethodon shenandoah* | Shenandoah Salamander | | | C |
| *Plethodon websteri* | Webster's Salamander | E | | |
| *Plethodon wehrlei* | Wehrle's Salamander | | C | – |
| *Plethodon welleri* | Weller's Salamander | | C | C |
| *Aneides aeneus* | Green Salamander | C | C | C |
| *Hyla andersoni* | Pine Barrens Treefrog | E | T | |
| *Hyla avivoca* | Bird-voiced Treefrog | C | | |
| *Rana areolata* | Crawfish Frog | – | C | |
| *Rana heckscheri* | River Frog | – | C | |
| *Alligator mississippiensis* | American Alligator | T | E | |
| *Clemmys guttata* | Spotted Turtle | C | – | – |
| *Clemmys muhlenbergi* | Bog Turtle | | C | C |
| *Gopherus polyphemus* | Gopher Tortoise | E | | |
| *Dermochelys coriacea* | Leatherback | E | E | E |
| *Chelonia mydas* | Green Turtle | E | E | E |
| *Eretmochelys imbricata* | Hawksbill | E | E | E |
| *Caretta caretta* | Loggerhead | T | E | E |
| *Lepidochelys kempi* | Ridley | E | E | E |
| *Eumeces anthracinus* | Coal Skink | T | C | – |
| *Pituophis melanoleucus* | Pine Snake | C | C | C |
| *Micrurus fulvius* | Eastern Coral Snake | C | C | |
| *Crotalus adamanteus* | Eastern Diamondback Rattlesnake | C | E | |

Endangered = E / Threatened = T / Concern = C / No immediate concern = –
Absent =

ploited without regard for the future and for the interests of others. Many laws have been passed in response to the growing awareness of the importance of natural resources: (1) Many years ago, song and game birds received federal protection, and this now extends to all but a few introduced avian species. (2) The taking of fur and game mammals is closely regulated by state laws. (3) Recently, many endangered plants and animals received federal and state protection. As yet, these laws embrace only a few species of amphibians and reptiles but many more will probably be included in the near future.

Legal restrictions also apply to the collecting of all organisms at state and federal parks (including the Blue Ridge Parkway), seashores, wildlife refuges, management areas, and (without permission) all private lands. Every naturalist—the serious student as well as the casual amateur—must respect the laws pertaining to the flora and fauna; however, it is not enough to observe merely the letter of the law. If collecting and field investigation (even those within the law) result in alteration of the environment, damage to segments of the biota can result. As near as possible, leave the habitat as you found it. Put back into its original location each rock, log, board, etc., that you moved. They offer shelter not only to amphibians and reptiles but to a host of other important organisms. Do not tear apart rotting logs with abandon or strip them of bark or moss, especially in areas used by the public. Keep in mind that many species are active at night and can then be collected with no disturbance to the habitat. In fact, under suitable atmospheric conditions, some species of amphibians can be seriously exploited at night. Limit your collecting to the minimum, take only as many animals as you can care for properly, and give every consideration for the future of the population. Avoid killing animals on the roads and encourage others to refrain from such senseless destruction of our fauna. In unpopulated areas, even venomous snakes should be left alone.

If an animal is to be kept as a pet, have proper quarters ready in advance, and remember that maintaining a pet is a responsibility, not a game. Provide cover, as most amphibians and reptiles are very secretive. Compared with birds and mammals, they require only occasional meals (usually once or twice a week is adequate), but many need warmth and moisture. Generally the common, readily available species are the easiest to maintain and observe. If you find that you cannot provide regular care for live animals, return them to their original habitat. Help to establish more rigid controls over commerce of the pet trade and hobbyists. Keep abreast of local, state, and federal issues related to natural resources, and take an informed and thoughtful position on those issues.

The species accounts are fairly standardized. First, the size range of adults is given: snout to vent for frogs, carapace length (straight line from anterior to posterior tip of carapace) for turtles, and total length (tip of snout to tip of tail) for all other groups. Metric measurements are used because, with the passage of legislation in 1975, the United States became committed to convert to that system within the next ten years. To smooth the transition, English approximations are given in parentheses. A brief description of the species follows, often with comments on features distinguishing the species from similar ones. In the next paragraph, the geographic range and the habitat are briefly described. This is followed by information on food habits, life history, and general biology. A color photograph of each species and a map showing its distribution within the area are provided. The text, photograph, and map for most species are all on one page, but for some species with unusual variation or interesting behavior, the accounts are longer and encompass two or three pages and usually two or three photographs. Because the sea turtles are strictly marine and come ashore only to lay eggs, maps of their ranges are omitted.

To facilitate finding information in the book, orders and families appear in phylogenetic sequence, genera and species in alphabetic order. Each class, order, and suborder is briefly described in an introductory account that includes comments on the local composition of that taxon.

To identify an amphibian or reptile, compare it with the photographs provided, select the ones that most closely match your specimen, and then carefully read the descriptions provided at the beginning of each account. Remember that just as persons differ, so do members of other species of animals. Therefore, do not be disturbed if your specimen differs slightly from the one pictured. Keep in mind, too, that individuals of many species often become darker (more melanistic) as they grow older. Also, be sure to check the maps because distribution is often an aid to identification, but remember that some geographic ranges are imperfectly known and that some are changing.

To confirm an identification or to report an extension of geographic range, write or visit the primary repository for herpetological information in your state: North Carolina State Museum of Natural History, Raleigh 27611; Charleston Museum, Charleston 29401; Virginia Herpetological Society, Box 1376, Leesburg 22075. Accompany all specimens with the following information: date of collection, precise location, brief description of habitat, name of collector, and possibly comments on behavior or activity.

Carefully study the photographs of the venomous snakes so that you can quickly identify these species in the field. Do not handle venomous snakes unless you must. Then be certain that you are adequately equipped and informed. Also, exercise caution in capturing turtles and large nonvenomous snakes; many will bite in self-defense.

### Acknowledgments

We thank the many individuals who made the preparation of this book so pleasant and enjoyable. A special debt of gratitude is due the many students who through the years encouraged this project not only with their general interest in amphibians and reptiles but also with their observations and collection of specimens. Much information was derived from specimens in the North Carolina State Museum of Natural History, Duke University, the Charleston Museum, and the Savannah Science Museum. We are grateful to those institutions for making their holdings available. The cooperation of Franklin J. Tobey, Jr., who made the records of the Virginia Herpetological Society available, and Robert H. Mount, who provided many unpublished records from South Carolina, is sincerely appreciated. We are especially grateful to Alvin L. Braswell, who has unstintingly assisted us in numerous ways. Very special thanks are extended to George, Robert, Paul, and June Tregembo for supplying many animals photographed in this publication, to Stephen G. Tilley for information and photographs of *Desmognathus imitator*, to Ray Ashton for the photograph of *Aneides aeneus*, and to Peter C. H. Pritchard and the Florida Audubon Society for photographs of three marine turtles. While space does not permit the listing of the many persons who have rendered assistance in various ways, we are especially in debt to Stanly Alford, Joseph M. Bauman, William S. Birkhead, E. E. Brown, Richard C. Bruce, E. D. Bruner, Mark Carawan, J. H. Carter III,

John E. Cooper, Floyd L. Downs, Navar Elliott, David A. Etnier, John B. Funderburg, Frank Groves, Richard L. Hoffman, C. R. Hoysa, R. B. Julian, the late Carl Kauffeld, Kenneth Kraeuter, Peter Marin, Sherman A. Minton, Jr., Joseph C. Mitchell, Philip Moran, James F. Parnell, Russell Peithman, Harvey Pough, William Redmond, Jerald H. Reynolds, J. K. Rose III, Albert E. Sanders, Frank J. Schwartz, F. F. Snelson, Jr., Mark Spinks, Wayne C. Starnes, David L. Stephan, K. C. Stone, Charles D. Sullivan, Joseph A. Travis, Henry M. Wilbur, Gerald Williamson, Gary Woodyard, and Thomas Yarbrough.

# The Area

## Introduction

Virginia and the Carolinas are highly diverse in topography, vegetation, and climate. As a consequence, the area has a remarkably rich fauna. Its nearly 324,000 square kilometers vary in aspect from sandy, barrier islands with maritime forests along the coast, and low, pine-covered ridges separated by floodplain forests or swamps farther inland, to relatively rugged mountains dominated primarily by northern hardwoods along the northwestern margin. In between these extremes is a broad, gently rolling plateau forested with oaks and pines.

Approximately 35 percent of the area is cultivated, and little of the remainder harbors forests such as those of precolonial times. No part of the area has escaped alteration, and most forests have been logged several times. Inland waters comprise only about 5 percent of the surface area. Rivers, streams, and swamps are relatively numerous, but there are few natural lakes such as Lake Drummond in southeastern Virginia and the bay lakes in southeastern North Carolina. In recent decades, however, several large impoundments have been constructed for hydroelectric power, recreation, and flood control; typical of these are the Santee-Cooper lakes in South Carolina and Kerr Reservoir along the border between North Carolina and Virginia.

The ranges of amphibians and reptiles are dynamic, not static, and are influenced by many complex factors. As environments change, ranges may also change. A knowledge of the more salient features of the area's physiography, vegetation, and climate is prerequisite to an understanding of the habitats and ranges occupied by particular species.

## Physiography

Portions of five physiographic provinces occur in the area (Fig. 1). As used here, the term *mountains* refers collectively to the higher elevations of the Appalachian plateau, Blue Ridge, and valley and ridge provinces. N. M. Fenneman's *Physiography of Eastern United*

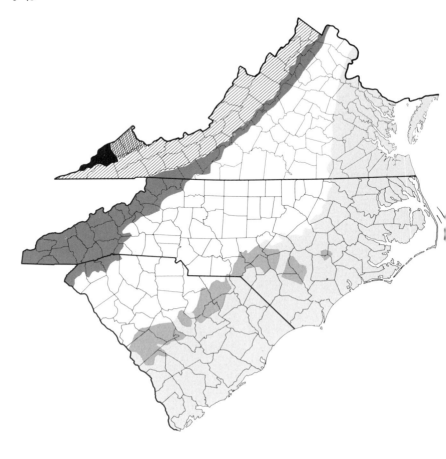

Appalachian Plateau
■ Cumberland Mountains
▨ Kanawha Plateau

▨ Ridge and Valley

■ Blue Ridge
□ Piedmont
□ Coastal Plain
■ Sandhills

*States*, published in 1938, is a useful reference for additional details concerning each province. The *Appalachian plateau* in extreme western Virginia is the smallest and consists of two different sections. The northeastern *Kanawha section* is a plateau with moderate to strong relief, whereas the southwestern *Cumberland Mountain section* is characterized by numerous deep valleys separated by steep, narrow ridges. Elevations average 600 m throughout the province, but range from 900 to 1,200 m in parts of the Cumberland Mountains. Many streams, tributaries of the Cumberland, Kentucky, and Big Sandy rivers, flow westward through the plateau west of our area. Extensive beds of coal underlie this province.

The *ridge and valley province* extends southwest to northeast along the northwestern margin of Virginia. In the southwest it abuts the Appalachian plateau, and on the east, the northernmost part of the Blue Ridge province. The ridge and valley province is a composite of six river valleys; the largest is the Shenandoah. The valleys are interspersed between elongate, parallel ridges 300 to 600 m in elevation. Massanutten Ridge, one of the highest, separates most of the Shenandoah Valley into two parts. Overall, the province is a highly folded, hilly region with a width of about 120 km in the north and about 80 km in the south. Sandstone, shale, and limestone are widespread and caves are numerous.

The *Blue Ridge province* is only several kilometers wide in the area north of Roanoke, Virginia. To the southwest, especially in North Carolina, it reaches a width of more than 80 km and is characterized by northeast-southwest-oriented ridges connected by a ladderlike series of cross ridges. Relief is rugged in places, accentuated by high peaks and steep, narrow gorges. The highest peaks occur in North Carolina where 82 exceed 1,525 m and 43 exceed 1,830 m. Mount Mitchell in the Black Mountain range reaches 2,037 m and is the highest peak in the eastern United States. South Carolina is the least mountainous of the three states; only its northwestern corner lies within the Blue Ridge province, where elevations vary from 300 to 600 m. The highest peak, Sassafras Mountain, reaches 1,083 m. In Virginia, most elevations are between 450 and 1,000 m; exceptions include the two highest peaks, Mount Rogers (1,743 m) and Whitetop Mountain (1,682 m). The Blue Ridge province is composed chiefly of granites and gneisses, and metamorphosed sedimentary rocks, principally siltstones, sandstones, and conglomerates. The continental divide generally extends along the eastern crest of the Blue Ridge province; streams originating on the western flank flow into the Gulf of Mexico, and those originating on the eastern flank flow into the Atlantic Ocean.

The *piedmont province* is a gently rolling plateau about 65 km wide in northern Virginia, 225 km wide at the Virginia-North Carolina border, and about 175 km wide in the Carolinas. Elevations decrease from 305–460 m in the northwest to 60–150 m in the southeast. It is the largest of the five provinces, including about 40 percent of the total area. The piedmont–Blue Ridge boundary is marked in places by steep escarpments through which rivers have cut deep, narrow gorges, especially in the Carolinas. The piedmont is delineated from the coastal plain by the fall line, a narrow zone marked chiefly by rapids formed in streams as they leave the crystalline bedrock of the piedmont and enter the coastal plain. Typically, there is no distinguishable change in relief at points of contact between the two provinces. While most of the piedmont consists of well-rounded hills and elongate, rolling ridges, it is punctuated by higher monadnocks, such as the Uwharrie and King's mountain ranges in North Carolina, and Parson's Mountain in South Carolina. The piedmont province is geologically older than the Blue Ridge province and is also underlain by complex igneous and metamorphic rocks.

The *Atlantic coastal plain province* includes about 10 percent of the land area in the continental United States, and approximately 38 percent of our area. Three major divisions are relatively distinct. The westernmost division, or *upper coastal plain*, extends eastward from the piedmont to the 84-m contour. It has a rolling topography and is generally well drained. A subdivision, the *sandhills*, characterized by deep, sandy soils, a rolling topography, and the highest elevations in the coastal plain, borders the fall line in South Carolina and in south-central North Carolina. The *middle coastal plain* lies between the 84-m and 29-m contours; it has a gently rolling topography and is also generally well drained. The easternmost division, or *lower coastal plain*, extends from the 29-m contour to sea level. This is a region of low relief, poor drainage, and numerous swamps. In southeastern Virginia, eastern North Carolina, and southeastern South Carolina, it is bordered by sandy outer banks or barrier islands. The coastal plain is underlain by geologically young, unconsolidated sedimentary formations that thicken from west to east. These are covered in most places by a relatively thin layer of sands and clays.

## Vegetation

The fully developed, or climax, vegetation of the Appalachian plateau is a highly diverse mixed hardwood forest on most slopes, with patches of spruce on the higher peaks and knobs. Bogs are numerous in valleys at the higher elevations, and open stands of pine exist in areas of sandy soil on the lower ridges.

Forests dominated by chestnut oak are prevalent throughout the ridge and valley province, especially on ridges and the upper slopes. Pines often occupy the drier sites, and mixed hardwoods occur in moist ravines and on the steeper northern slopes. Where not farmed, valley floors harbor forests dominated by oaks and tulip-poplars with dogwood as an important understory species. Red cedar is often present in limestone areas.

The Blue Ridge has the most diverse vegetation of the provinces in the area. Several types of deciduous hardwood forests are present, and stands of spruce or fir occur on many peaks which exceed 1,370 m. A highly diverse cove hardwoods forest occupies sheltered valleys, protected lower slopes, and relatively open north- or east-facing slopes, at elevations of 460 m to 1,370 m. Most stands contain 25 to 30 species, and are similar to the mixed hardwood forests of the Appalachian plateau and portions of the ridge and valley province. Hemlock forests occur along streams at lower elevations and in some moist ravines at higher elevations. These usually are not pure stands but contain various hardwoods such as sugar maple and Fraser's magnolia. Dense thickets of rhododendron at the borders of streams are also characteristic. The more exposed slopes up to elevations of 1,370 m to 1,525 m are generally occupied by oak forests. A shrub layer is usually present, but varies in thickness and in species composition; common understory species include dogwood and sourwood. Until the 1920s, chestnut was codominant with the oaks throughout the Appalachians. However, the chestnut succumbed to the attack of an introduced blight fungus and, except for occasional saplings growing from old stumps, is now absent.

On most dry, open ridges, and on steep, open south- or southwest-facing slopes, pines replace hardwoods, especially at lower elevations. From southwestern Virginia throughout much of western North Carolina, stands of spruce or fir are found at elevations above 1,370 m. When destroyed by fire, wind damage, or cutting, the spruce-fir association is replaced by an early successional stage

*Mountain ridges with pine forests*

dominated by mountain ash, yellow birch, and fire cherry. On steep south-facing gaps between stands of fir or spruce, beech orchards may be present, while at lower elevations on steep, exposed slopes with relatively rugged relief, extensive heath balds dominated by rhododendron and mountain laurel often develop. Throughout the southern portion of this province, open grassy areas, or grass balds, usually surrounded by forests, are common on southern, southwestern, and western exposures at elevations of 1,585 m to 1,770 m.

Except on the wettest and driest sites, most upland portions of the piedmont province were covered by oak-hickory forests with understories of dogwood, sourwood, and other species. On the drier sites, pines prevailed, and along rivers and streams were narrow corridors of bottomland hardwoods with thick understories of cane. On some moist, steep, north-facing slopes, usually near streams, mixed hardwood forests similar to those of the Blue Ridge province occurred. Stands of hemlock were also present in some areas, usually on bluffs along streams. Until the colonial period, at least in South Carolina, open prairielike tracts dominated by stands of cane 1.5 m to 9 m tall occurred on some piedmont ridges. Although remnants of most of these early associations persist, much of the province is under cultivation or occupied by stands of second- or third-growth oaks and pines.

Pine forests of various kinds dominate most of the coastal plain

*Heath bald with rhododendron*

province, particularly on the more elevated, sandier, and drier sites. If forest fires are infrequent, hardwoods replace pines on the moister sites. In the southern and more coastal portions of the province, a mixed evergreen hardwood association is the climax forest type. Farther north and in more inland areas, deciduous hardwoods replace evergreens as the dominant species. On dry, sandy sites with a rolling topography, relatively open stands of longleaf pine and turkey oak are common. The herb layer of these stands is dominated by clumps of wire grass interspersed between bare patches of white or pale yellow sand. On gently sloping ridges, or on extensive, poorly drained areas with little relief, pine savannas or flatwoods often develop. These are characterized by loblolly or longleaf pines with a continuous, highly diverse herb layer of grasses and other flowering plants. Wire grass sometimes grows on the better-drained sites.

Scattered throughout upland pine savannas or flatwoods are numerous evergreen shrub bogs (also called bays or pocosins). These are often circular or elliptical, variable in size, and are commonly bordered by dense thickets of evergreen shrubs such as sweet bay, loblolly bay, gallberry, and sweet pepper-bush. Pond pine is frequently present. All of these plants may occur in the interior as well as at the margins of the bogs. Evergreen shrub bogs are usually wet throughout most of the year, but surface waters may be hidden by mats of sphagnum moss or other plants. Cypress

*Sandhills*

*Pine flatwoods*

*Evergreen shrub bog*

or gum ponds are also characteristic of upland pine savannas or flatwoods. In these ponds the herb and shrub layers are sparse or absent; cypresses dominate if water is present throughout most of the year, while gums dominate if water availability is seasonal.

Bottomland or swamp forests occur along rivers and the larger streams. The floodplains of black-water rivers or streams, and flat areas associated with upland drainage channels, are dominated by cypress or gum. Cypress is prevalent in areas where the soil rarely dries. The floodplains of major rivers originating in the piedmont or mountain regions usually have hardwood forests. Distinctive maritime forests characterized by evergreen oaks, hollies, red bay, and pines occur on the outer banks and barrier islands. Cabbage palmetto is a conspicuous dominant on most barrier islands in South Carolina. Behind the primary dunes on many barrier islands, a nearly impenetrable thicket of yaupon holly, wax myrtle, red cedar, and greenbrier borders the forest.

Additional details concerning most of the habitats discussed above may be found in the *North Carolina Atlas,* edited by J. W. Clay, D. M. Orr, Jr., and A. W. Stuart (University of North Carolina Press, 1975).

*Cypress-gum association*

*Maritime forest*

## Climate

The area's climate is variable and changes from a pattern of cold winters and relatively mild summers in the north and in the mountains to one of mild winters and hot summers in the south and on the coast. Coastal areas are subject to the modifying influence of the adjacent Atlantic Ocean, while the more variable patterns of the mountains are dependent on local differences in topography and relief. Piedmont localities typically have cold to moderately cold winters and hot summers, with the severity of winter weather increasing toward the north and the west. Phenological events such as the initiation of breeding activity in salamanders generally occur earlier at lower elevations and more southern latitudes than at higher elevations and more northern latitudes.

In the coastal plain, annual precipitation averages 100–120 cm in the north and 115–135 cm in the south; the highest amounts occur in North Carolina. Precipitation is more variable in the mountains, averaging 80–125 cm in the north and 100–215 cm in the south. The highest averages occur in the southern mountains, particularly in the Great Smokies, the Nantahalas, and the Blue Ridge escarpment along the western border of the Carolinas. Rainfall in these areas may exceed 255 cm per year. Precipitation in the piedmont is generally intermediate between that of the mountains and the coastal plain. For the area as a whole, most rain occurs in mid-summer; the least occurs in the fall, and moderately high amounts occur in winter and spring. Piedmont summers are generally dry. Winter snowfall is frequent in mountain and piedmont areas, but mountain peaks lack snowcaps during summer months.

Average temperatures are variable in the mountains, but relatively uniform in the piedmont and the coastal plain. In the coastal plain, January averages range from 2.2–5.6°C in the north to 8.9–10.0°C in the south. For mountain localities, the range is 0–3.3°C in the north to 1.1–5.6°C in the south. In the coastal plain, July averages range from 25.6°C in the north to 26.7°C or above in the south. For the mountains, the range is 20.0–23.3°C at most localities. Piedmont averages closely approximate those of the coastal plain.

Coastal areas receive the potentially devastating effects of hurricanes from June to November, most often in September. The coast of the eastern United States endures about five hurricanes in an average year.

# History of the Herpetofauna
# of the Carolinas and Virginia

Three factors have combined to make the herpetological history of
our area a rich one. The first is historical—the seaboard of these
states was explored and colonized early, as early as more northern
states and earlier than those of the south. The second factor is
biological, the fauna itself, numerous in species and individuals,
is three times the size of that of New England, and twice that to be
found from Delaware northward and includes such spectacular
elements as alligators, sea turtles, rattlesnakes, congo eels, and
vociferous and colorful frogs, all of which were duly reported in
early travelers' accounts, sometimes faithfully and sometimes with
the colorful embellishment of folklore.

The final factor is one of chance, the human element, in which
three men figured most prominently, Mark Catesby in the pre-
Linnaean era, Dr. Alexander Garden, a collaborator of Linnaeus in
the 1760s, and Dr. John Holbrook, who wrote the first compre-
hensive North American herpetology nearly a century later, all of
whom chose Charleston as a home base.

Our herpetofaunal history began almost with the earliest settle-
ments. The colonization of our states coincided with a burgeoning
interest in natural history in Europe where individuals and local
societies were avidly collecting seeds, plants, and animal curiosities for their gardens and private collections. Under the influence
of such naturalists as John Ray in seventeenth-century England
and Carolus Linnaeus of Sweden in the next century, travelers
and local correspondents were encouraged to send natural history
specimens back for cultivation and study. Growing interests in
medicine, pharmacology, and new food sources were important
stimuli, as was curiosity about natural science per se.

Our history divides naturally into two major phases. The first
embraced the colonial period and the first years of the nineteenth
century, a time of exploration and discovery, the results of which
were reported by European naturalists in the European press and
at scientific meetings. This period could be divided into pre- and
post-Linnaean, but such a division would recognize only the for-
mality of binominal nomenclature following Linnaeus. Neither

the direction nor the quality of natural history research changed appreciably.

After a virtual hiatus of a quarter century, during which national intellectual and scientific seeds were germinating, the second phase began when the rising school of American naturalists took over from their overseas colleagues. They announced their findings at meetings and in the journals of newly founded American societies. This phase is divided loosely into two periods. The first extends from about 1830 to World War II when scientific research emphasized anatomy and development and, with the advent of Darwin's influence, evolutionary relationships. After World War II the emphasis shifted to ecological and behavioral approaches.

The early colonial period was largely a recording of travelers' tales of encounters with the local animals interspersed with the legends and beliefs surrounding them. The Reverend John Bannister of Virginia (d. 1692) told the tale of the rattlesnake, which by the power of its stare forced a squirrel to descend a tree to be eaten. Robert Beverly, in *The History and Present State of Virginia* (London, 1705), commented on several herpetological subjects: the noise made by croaking frogs, the size and "roaring" of bullfrogs, the rattlesnake (which he never saw in life), and several other snakes. He almost correctly asserted that the venomous snakes bear living young whereas other sorts lay eggs. The striking of a gun butt by the sharp tail of a horn snake with such force as to engage the butt and the charming of birds and squirrels by snakes are among his anecdotes. He also told of a rattlesnake encountered in the process of swallowing a squirrel, the other end of which was taken by a dog that pulled until the snake gave up. The dog ate the squirrel and the raconteur ate the snake "which was dainty food," perhaps the first account of what was to become an exotic hors d'oeuvre for the adventurous gourmet two and a half centuries later.

The first really significant account of the herpetofauna of our area is that of John Lawson, surveyor, naturalist, and outdoorsman, whose *A New Voyage to Carolina* (London, 1709; reprinted as the *History of Carolina*, London, 1714) was based on his travels and experiences a few years earlier. His list, "Insects of Carolina," included the alligator, about twenty kinds of snakes, three lizards, a tortoise and terrapin, "many sorts" of frogs, and the "Eel-snake" (*Amphiuma*). At that time the terms insect and reptile referred to crawling creatures rather than to particular animal groups, and Lawson simply reversed our present usage. Beyond his list he devoted about ten pages to a discussion, species by species, of their biology, dangers, uses, etc., much of it accurately reporting personal observations. He gave a dramatic account of a large alligator in late March that started bellowing about nine in the evening from its hibernating burrow directly beneath his cabin on the river bank. An Indian companion returned shortly after the episode to explain the source of the noise to the badly frightened Lawson. He added a description of the eggs and commented on the use of alligator flesh for food and for its medicinal properties.

Lawson's care as an observer is revealed in his descriptions of the rattle and teeth of the rattlesnake, but his credulity is also unmasked by his acceptance of its power to charm and the curative virtues of its cast skin, rattle, and gall. His comments on the remainder of the fauna are an equally amusing mixture of fact and fiction. Lawson had planned an extensive study of the natural history of Carolina, but he was murdered by Indians in 1711.

For nearly a century other travelers recorded notes and anecdotes of a similar nature, often cribbed from Lawson, and seldom adding significant new information. Likewise, many serious naturalists including John and William Bartram, Alexander Wilson, and John LeConte passed through, but their herpetological observations in our area were very minor.

The most outstanding figure of the pre-Linnaean era was Mark Catesby, whose monumental *The Natural History of Carolina, Florida and the Bahama Islands* (2 volumes, London 1731–43) was in its time the most elaborate and ambitious study in natural history of the New World. The first volume was devoted principally to birds with descriptions and full page paintings with natural backgrounds where the flora is shown. The second volume includes a fair representation of the herpetofauna similarly treated as well as mammals and some marine fishes and invertebrates.

Catesby, at age twenty-seven, interested but not greatly experienced in natural history, went to Virginia in 1712 to stay for a time with his sister and her husband, Dr. William Cocke, who had migrated a few years earlier to become a prosperous pioneer of Virginia medicine and an early figure in the social and political life of Williamsburg. Here Catesby met William Byrd who hosted him and encouraged his naturalistic pursuits, and who introduced him to other prominent persons who were to aid his endeavors. He collected botanical specimens for Samuel Dale and perhaps other gardeners and nurserymen in England. He spent most of his early stay in the tidewater regions of Virginia, but he did ascend the James River to the mountains and in 1714 made a voyage to the West Indies. Little is known of his activities during the next five years, prior to his return to England in the autumn of 1719, but lasting impressions had been made, he had gained New World experience, and he had made some bird drawings.

After considerable planning and uncertainty, Catesby returned to America in 1722 with the blessings of the Royal Society and the financial backing of some of its members who hoped for returns in the form of botanical materials and natural history curiosities. On his part Catesby's aim was to study the flora and fauna of the country and prepare illustrations for a book on its natural history. He settled in Charles Town (now Charleston) with the inducement of £20 a year authorized by the governor of Carolina. He remained there over two years interspersed with several expeditions into the piedmont.

The Florida component of Catesby's work is vague, and it seems he himself did not engage in field work south of the Savannah area. But regional names at that time lacked the precision they merit today. He visited the Bahamas in 1725 where he concentrated on marine life, but he did draw and describe three lizards and one snake of West Indian species. All the other reptiles and amphibians depicted are species found in the general vicinity of Charleston: one salamander, four frogs, three lizards, eighteen snakes, and four sea turtles. The majority of these can be identified as species recognized today, but a few snakes are possibly composite such as the "Black Viper" which combines characters of the Cottonmouth and the Eastern Hognose Snake, neither of which are otherwise certainly represented. Many of Catesby's accounts were later incorporated in the binominal descriptions of species by Linnaeus and post-Linnaean authors, who, because our scientific nomenclature dates from the tenth edition of *Systema Naturae* (1758), are credited with the original descriptions rather than Catesby.

In the tenth edition of *Systema Naturae*, only two species of reptiles and amphibians were included that are thought to have been based on specimens from our area, the Five-lined Skink and the Eastern Box Turtle. When, in 1766, the next (twelfth) edition appeared, it included thirteen additional new species from Carolina. The difference was due to the efforts of Dr. Alexander Garden, a young Scotch physician who immigrated to Charleston in 1752. Dr. Garden practiced medicine for almost thirty years until he was forced to return to Britain in 1782 as a consequence of his loyalist sympathies. However, during his years in the American colony his great love and avocation was natural history, and he sent to his scientific colleagues in Europe quantities of seed and seedlings, and to Linnaeus many preserved specimens of fishes, amphibians, and reptiles. The only species name credited to Garden himself is *Amphiuma means*, which acquired scientific status in 1821 with the posthumous publication of his correspondence with Linnaeus. His specimen and letters describing it had arrived too late for inclusion in the *Systema Naturae* of 1766. Most of his few and scattered publications dealt with medical subjects, but his extensive correspondence with British and other European naturalists as well as the drawings and collections he sent did much to promote knowledge of our flora and fauna. Garden was responsible for first notices of such genuine novelties as the Greater Siren, the Congo Eel, and the Florida Softshell.

Between 1789 and 1803 a further nineteen now recognized species from our area, predominantly frogs and turtles, were added by no less than eleven authors from a variety of sources. This flurry marks the end of European domination of American natural sciences in general and of Carolina herpetology in particular. Other than the *Amphiuma* mentioned above, only one final species, the Carolina Anole was described by a European, Voigt, in 1832.

In 1822 Dr. John Edwards Holbrook settled in Charleston to practice medicine, just as had Alexander Garden seventy years earlier. Holbrook was a South Carolinian by birth, but had been raised in New England and educated at Brown University, University of Pennsylvania, Edinburgh, and Paris, where a stay at the Jardin des Plantes brought him in contact with leading figures in biology who were influential in determining his later direction in natural history. Shortly after his arrival in Charleston, he became first professor of anatomy (1824) at the Medical College of the State of South Carolina, and about the same time he began work on *North American Herpetology*, destined to become a classic. The first edition appeared in four volumes (1836–40), but Holbrook was not pleased with it, and nearly all the copies were recalled to be replaced with a second edition in 1842, in five volumes. Only four complete sets of the first edition are known to exist, and a good set of the second edition would bring several thousand dollars today. The five volumes total nearly 700 pages with 147 individual accounts, most of them illustrated in color from living specimens.

Although the work was intended to cover the herpetofauna of the whole country, then made up of twenty-five states, his Charleston focus and the cultural heritage of the eastern seaboard assured that the fauna of the Carolinas and Virginia figured prominently. Nearly 60 percent of Holbrook's species were recognized to occur in these states, which today have just over a third of the recognized species of the present coterminous United States.

Perhaps not surprisingly, the herpetology of the area was due for a period of relative inactivity following Holbrook's masterpiece. Between then and the advent of the twentieth century another half dozen species were described from our fauna by Edward D. Cope and others, and the late nineteenth century saw the completion of Cope's great monographs, the *Batrachia* (1889) and the posthumous *Reptilia* (1900), which updated the field for the country as a whole but had no local emphasis.

In late 1880 the Brimley brothers immigrated from England to North Carolina to devote their long lives to North Carolina's natural history. H. H. Brimley headed the new state museum in Raleigh, concentrating his efforts in ornithology and conservation. C. S. Brimley became an entomologist with the Department of Agriculture, to which field he contributed extensively and well. In addition he became the state's leading authority on herpetology. Between 1895 and 1939 he published forty-seven papers dealing with many aspects of the state's herpetofauna including identification and description, ecology, behavior, and seasonal distribution. In the period 1939–43, he published a series of summary papers in *Carolina Tips,* and these were later brought together in a pamphlet that comprises the first herpetology of the state, published by the Carolina Biological Supply Company.

E. Burnham Chamberlain played a similar role in South Carolina herpetology. A naturalist from boyhood, he joined the staff of the Charleston Museum in 1924 as curator of vertebrate zoology and began an active research career. He is coauthor of *South Carolina Bird Life* and is best known as an ornithologist, but he contributed several valuable papers on amphibians and reptiles of South Carolina. He is largely responsible for the nucleus of the herpetological collection of the museum. Perhaps his greatest contribution is the inspiration he provided a generation ago to a sizable group of Charleston youngsters who are making their mark today as leading herpetologists. As emeritus curator of vertebrate zoology, Chamberlain continues to be active professionally today.

Another contemporary who was to have a major impact on the regional herpetofauna was Emmett Reid Dunn, a young Virginian, who, early in his career, specialized in salamanders. No other area of the world comes close to having the diversity and abundance of salamanders that our area boasts. The publication of Dunn's *Salamanders of the Family Plethodontidae* in 1926 proved a tremendous stimulus to others to investigate this group. His book brought together a difficult literature in a convenient and thorough manner and called attention to the problems and the importance of the southern Appalachians as a center of abundance and diversification for this largest salamander family. The advent of the automobile and highway network must be recognized as a major factor in exploiting the salamander fauna of these mountains since many of the distributions are so remarkably restricted that only in the present generation have several species been discovered.

As the contributors to our herpetological history changed, so also did the character of their contributions. The colonial period was naturally one of exploration and inventory. What sort of animals inhabited this new land? What were they good for or what hazards did they present? Descriptions and folklore embellished the lists, and gradually more accurate observations on natural history and behavior were added.

In the nineteenth century the emphasis passed to anatomy and evolutionary relationships in keeping with prevailing trends in biology. These classical disciplines are still in vogue and being pursued actively with the addition of new biochemical and microscopic techniques. The mainstream of present-day investigations is in population biology: community structure, species interactions, and the role of reptiles and amphibians in the ecosystem. Environmental preservation has become a public concern; we hope in time to save some of our more precarious species from the fate of the Passenger Pigeon, Carolina Parokeet, and Ivory-billed Woodpecker.

Space does not permit mention of the many competent persons now engaged in study of our herpetofauna. Most of the major universities as well as the Charleston Museum, North Carolina State Museum, the Norfolk Museum, and the Highlands (North Carolina) and Mountain Lake (Virginia) biological stations are actively sponsoring education and research in the field. The Virginia Herpetological Society is a predominantly amateur group contributing to our knowledge of the distribution and habits of the local fauna. A similar organization for North Carolina has just been formed.

For further information on herpetological history see: (1) *Dr. Alexander Garden of Charles Town* by David Berkeley and Dorothy Smith Berkeley (University of North Carolina Press, 1969); (2) *Mark Catesby the Colonial Audubon* by George Frederick Frick and Raymond Phineas Stearns (University of Illinois Press, 1961); and (3) *North American Herpetology* by John Edwards Holbrook (provided with a biographical sketch and technical updating, the second edition was reprinted by the Society for the Study of Amphibians and Reptiles, 1976).

# List of Amphibians and Reptiles of the Carolinas and Virginia

**Class Amphibia**

ORDER CAUDATA = URODELA

Cryptobranchidae
    *Cryptobranchus alleganiensis*     Hellbender
Sirenidae
    *Pseudobranchus striatus*     Dwarf Siren
    *Siren intermedia*     Lesser Siren
    *Siren lacertina*     Greater Siren
Salamandridae
    *Notophthalmus viridescens*     Eastern Newt
Proteidae
    *Necturus lewisi*     Carolina Mudpuppy
    *Necturus maculosus*     Common Mudpuppy
    *Necturus punctatus*     Dwarf Mudpuppy
Amphiumidae
    *Amphiuma means*     Two-toed Amphiuma
Ambystomatidae
    *Ambystoma cingulatum*     Flatwoods Salamander
    *Ambystoma jeffersonianum*     Jefferson Salamander
    *Ambystoma mabeei*     Mabee's Salamander
    *Ambystoma maculatum*     Spotted Salamander
    *Ambystoma opacum*     Marbled Salamander
    *Ambystoma talpoideum*     Mole Salamander
    *Ambystoma tigrinum*     Tiger Salamander
Plethodontidae
    *Aneides aeneus*     Green Salamander
    *Desmognathus aeneus*     Cherokee Salamander
    *Desmognathus auriculatus*     Southern Dusky Salamander
    *Desmognathus fuscus*     Northern Dusky Salamander
    *Desmognathus imitator*     Imitator Salamander
    *Desmognathus monticola*     Seal Salamander

| | |
|---|---|
| *Desmognathus ochrophaeus* | Mountain Dusky Salamander |
| *Desmognathus quadramaculatus* | Blackbelly Salamander |
| *Desmognathus welteri* | Cumberland Salamander |
| *Desmognathus wrighti* | Pigmy Salamander |
| *Eurycea bislineata* | Two-lined Salamander |
| *Eurycea guttolineata* | Three-lined Salamander |
| *Eurycea junaluska* | Junaluska Salamander |
| *Eurycea longicauda* | Longtail Salamander |
| *Eurycea lucifuga* | Cave Salamander |
| *Eurycea quadridigitata* | Dwarf Salamander |
| *Gyrinophilus porphyriticus* | Spring Salamander |
| *Hemidactylium scutatum* | Four-toed Salamander |
| *Leurognathus marmoratus* | Shovelnose Salamander |
| *Plethodon cinereus* | Redback Salamander |
| *Plethodon dorsalis* | Zigzag Salamander |
| *Plethodon glutinosus* | Slimy Salamander |
| *Plethodon hoffmani* | Valley and Ridge Salamander |
| *Plethodon hubrichti* | Peaks of Otter Salamander |
| *Plethodon jordani* | Jordan's Salamander |
| *Plethodon punctatus* | Cow Knob Salamander |
| *Plethodon richmondi* | Ravine Salamander |
| *Plethodon serratus* | Southern Redback Salamander |
| *Plethodon shenandoah* | Shenandoah Salamander |
| *Plethodon websteri* | Webster's Salamander |
| *Plethodon wehrlei* | Wehrle's Salamander |
| *Plethodon welleri* | Weller's Salamander |
| *Plethodon yonahlossee* | Yonahlossee Salamander |
| *Pseudotriton montanus* | Mud Salamander |
| *Pseudotriton ruber* | Red Salamander |
| *Stereochilus marginatus* | Many-lined Salamander |

ORDER SALIENTIA = ANURA

Pelobatidae

| | |
|---|---|
| *Scaphiopus holbrooki* | Eastern Spadefoot Toad |

Bufonidae

| | |
|---|---|
| *Bufo americanus* | American Toad |
| *Bufo quercicus* | Oak Toad |
| *Bufo terrestris* | Southern Toad |
| *Bufo woodhousei* | Fowler's Toad |

Hylidae

| | |
|---|---|
| *Acris crepitans* | Northern Cricket Frog |
| *Acris gryllus* | Southern Cricket Frog |
| *Hyla andersoni* | Pine Barrens Treefrog |
| *Hyla avivoca* | Bird-voiced Treefrog |
| *Hyla chrysoscelis* | Cope's Gray Treefrog |
| *Hyla cinerea* | Green Treefrog |
| *Hyla crucifer* | Spring Peeper |
| *Hyla femoralis* | Pine Woods Treefrog |
| *Hyla gratiosa* | Barking Treefrog |
| *Hyla squirella* | Squirrel Treefrog |
| *Hyla versicolor* | Gray Treefrog |
| *Limnaoedus ocularis* | Little Grass Frog |
| *Pseudacris brachyphona* | Mountain Chorus Frog |
| *Pseudacris brimleyi* | Brimley's Chorus Frog |
| *Pseudacris nigrita* | Southern Chorus Frog |
| *Pseudacris ornata* | Ornate Chorus Frog |
| *Pseudacris triseriata* | Upland Chorus Frog |

Ranidae

| | |
|---|---|
| *Rana areolata* | Crawfish Frog |
| *Rana catesbeiana* | Bullfrog |
| *Rana clamitans* | Green Frog |
| *Rana grylio* | Pig Frog |
| *Rana heckscheri* | River Frog |
| *Rana palustris* | Pickerel Frog |
| *Rana sphenocephala* | Southern Leopard Frog |
| *Rana sylvatica* | Wood Frog |
| *Rana virgatipes* | Carpenter Frog |

Microhylidae

| | |
|---|---|
| *Gastrophryne carolinensis* | Eastern Narrowmouth Toad |

## Class Reptilia

ORDER CROCODILIA = LORICATA

Crocodilidae

| | |
|---|---|
| *Alligator mississippiensis* | American Alligator |

ORDER CHELONIA = TESTUDINATA

Chelydridae
   *Chelydra serpentina* — Snapping Turtle
Kinosternidae
   *Kinosternon subrubrum* — Eastern Mud Turtle
   *Sternotherus minor* — Stripeneck Musk Turtle
   *Sternotherus odoratus* — Eastern Musk Turtle
Emydidae
   *Chrysemys concinna* — River Cooter
   *Chrysemys floridana* — Florida Cooter
   *Chrysemys picta* — Painted Turtle
   *Chrysemys rubriventris* — Redbelly Turtle
   *Chrysemys scripta* — Yellowbelly Slider
   *Clemmys guttata* — Spotted Turtle
   *Clemmys insculpta* — Wood Turtle
   *Clemmys muhlenbergi* — Bog Turtle
   *Deirochelys reticularia* — Chicken Turtle
   *Graptemys geographica* — Map Turtle
   *Malaclemys terrapin* — Diamondback Terrapin
   *Terrapene carolina* — Eastern Box Turtle
Testudinidae
   *Gopherus polyphemus* — Gopher Tortoise
Dermochelyidae
   *Dermochelys coriacea* — Leatherback
Cheloniidae
   *Caretta caretta* — Loggerhead
   *Chelonia mydas* — Green Turtle
   *Eretmochelys imbricata* — Hawksbill
   *Lepidochelys kempi* — Ridley
Trionychidae
   *Trionyx ferox* — Florida Softshell
   *Trionyx spiniferus* — Spiny Softshell

ORDER SQUAMATA

*Suborder Sauria = Lacertilia*
Iguanidae
   *Anolis carolinensis* — Carolina Anole
   *Phrynosoma cornutum* — Texas Horned Lizard
   *Sceloporus undulatus* — Eastern Fence Lizard

Scincidae
  *Eumeces anthracinus*       Coal Skink
  *Eumeces fasciatus*         Five-lined Skink
  *Eumeces inexpectatus*      Southeastern
                              Five-lined Skink
  *Eumeces laticeps*          Broadhead Skink
  *Scincella lateralis*       Ground Skink
Teiidae
  *Cnemidophorus sexlineatus*  Six-lined Racerunner
Anguidae
  *Ophisaurus attenuatus*     Slender Glass Lizard
  *Ophisaurus compressus*     Island Glass Lizard
  *Ophisaurus ventralis*      Eastern Glass Lizard

*Suborder Serpentes = Ophidia*

Colubridae
  *Carphophis amoenus*        Worm Snake
  *Cemophora coccinea*        Scarlet Snake
  *Coluber constrictor*       Black Racer
  *Diadophis punctatus*       Ringneck Snake
  *Elaphe guttata*            Corn Snake
  *Elaphe obsoleta*           Rat Snake
  *Farancia abacura*          Mud Snake
  *Farancia erytrogramma*     Rainbow Snake
  *Heterodon platyrhinos*     Eastern Hognose Snake
  *Heterodon simus*           Southern Hognose Snake
  *Lampropeltis calligaster*  Mole Kingsnake
  *Lampropeltis getulus*      Eastern Kingsnake
  *Lampropeltis triangulum*   Eastern Milk Snake and
                              Scarlet Kingsnake
  *Masticophis flagellum*     Eastern Coachwhip
  *Nerodia cyclopion*         Green Water Snake
  *Nerodia erythrogaster*     Redbelly Water Snake
  *Nerodia fasciata*          Banded Water Snake
  *Nerodia sipedon*           Northern Water Snake
  *Nerodia taxispilota*       Brown Water Snake
  *Opheodrys aestivus*        Rough Green Snake
  *Opheodrys vernalis*        Smooth Green Snake
  *Pituophis melanoleucus*    Pine Snake
  *Regina rigida*             Glossy Crayfish Snake
  *Regina septemvittata*      Queen Snake

| | |
|---|---|
| *Rhadinaea flavilata* | Pine Woods Snake |
| *Seminatrix pygaea* | Black Swamp Snake |
| *Storeria dekayi* | Brown Snake |
| *Storeria occipitomaculata* | Redbelly Snake |
| *Tantilla coronata* | Southeastern Crowned Snake |
| *Thamnophis sauritus* | Eastern Ribbon Snake |
| *Thamnophis sirtalis* | Eastern Garter Snake |
| *Virginia striatula* | Rough Earth Snake |
| *Virginia valeriae* | Smooth Earth Snake |

Elapidae
| | |
|---|---|
| *Micrurus fulvius* | Eastern Coral Snake |

Crotalidae
| | |
|---|---|
| *Agkistrodon contortrix* | Copperhead |
| *Agkistrodon piscivorus* | Cottonmouth |
| *Crotalus adamanteus* | Eastern Diamondback Rattlesnake |
| *Crotalus horridus* | Timber Rattlesnake |
| *Sistrurus miliarius* | Pigmy Rattlesnake |

# Class Amphibia

Amphibians evolved from fish during late Devonian times and became the first land-dwelling vertebrates. They are the ancestors of other tetrapods (reptiles, birds, and mammals). Even today, amphibians are of major biological importance. They avidly eat insects and are eagerly eaten by many organisms. Their hardiness, small size, low metabolism, and simple environmental needs make them excellent experimental animals. In this capacity, they have contributed greatly to our understanding of embryology, anatomy, tissue regeneration, physiology, and behavior.

Most amphibians are four-legged, have a smooth, moist skin, lack scales, lay shell-less eggs in freshwater or in moist places on land, have an aquatic larval stage, and are quasi-terrestrial as adults. The term *Amphibia* is derived from Greek and means "both life" in reference to the ability of many species to live on land and in water.

Our amphibian fauna is totally indigenous. No species has been successfully introduced, but some species have been transported within the area, primarily for use as fish bait. The major disruptive factor has been human technological encroachment. Many species have been eliminated from parts of our area, but, by the same token, a few have prospered, e.g., with the extensive construction of farm ponds. The living amphibians of our area include the two major orders: Caudata (salamanders) and Salientia (frogs and toads).

## Order Caudata = Urodela

SALAMANDERS

Salamanders have elongated bodies. The long trunk and tail provide the chief locomotor thrust when swimming, whereas their small limbs permit crawling on land. Some of our salamanders (Cherokee and Pigmy) become adults when only about 44 mm long, but others (Hellbender, Greater Siren, and Two-toed Amphiuma) approach or exceed 1 m. Most are about 125 mm long.

Almost all salamanders are voiceless. The chemical messengers (pheromones) secreted by hedonic glands evoke courtship and spawning behavior. Fertilization is external in the Hellbender and probably in the Sirens. In all other species it is internal. The male deposits a packet of sperm on a gelatinous stalk (spermatophore), and the female clasps the packet with her cloaca.

Salamanders typically undergo an aquatic larval stage lasting from a few days to several years, but in some plethodontids the larval stage is completed within the egg membrane prior to hatching. The larval stage ends with metamorphosis, a series of definitive changes in structure and life cycle. Adults of some species retain numerous larval features; the Sirens and Mudpuppies are classical examples. Some species are totally aquatic, many live in moist places on land but go to the water to breed, and others are completely terrestrial. Surprisingly few are arboreal; possibly that habitat is too hostile even though western North Carolina has unusually high rainfall. Much variation in respiration also occurs. Some species have lungs but retain gills throughout life (Sirens and Mudpuppies), others with lungs retain only the gill slits (Hellbender and Amphiuma), and still others (family Plethodontidae) lack both lungs and gills and respire mainly via the skin. Most salamanders feed on all small, moving organisms available in their habitats, but some show strong preferences, e.g., the Spring Salamander prefers smaller salamanders.

The order Caudata includes about 320 species, a very small proportion of the world fauna. Many families inhabit the north temperate zone but only one family (Plethodontidae) is successful in the tropics (New World). The Carolinas and Virginia have a relatively rich salamander fauna containing 52 species. Most occur in the mountains, unlike the other amphibians and reptiles which have their greatest species diversity in the coastal plain (Table I). Our salamanders generally have small geographic ranges and a high degree of endemism. Four species are endemic and 11 others have over two-thirds of their ranges within the area. Only 5 species occur areawide. In contrast to the 30 percent endemism shown by the Caudata, the Salientia exhibit about 10 percent and the Reptilia none.

Most (36) of our salamanders are plethodontids—a dominant family with nine genera, three of which are large: *Plethodon* (14 species), *Desmognathus* (9), and *Eurycea* (6). The only other large group is the Ambystomatidae, a family with seven species all in the genus *Ambystoma*. Nonetheless, our fauna is taxonomically diverse; three other families and also six genera are each represented by only 1 species.

**Hellbender** *Cryptobranchus alleganiensis*

300 to 740 mm (12 to 29 in.) "Ugly, slimy, and large" best describes this grayish brown salamander. The flat head bears small, lidless eyes. The legs are short and stout, and a large wrinkled fold of skin extends along the side of the body. Adults lack gills but have a gill slit on each side of the throat.

Hellbenders live mainly in streams of the Mississippi drainage in the western part of our area. They prefer large, clear, fast-flowing streams with big, flat rocks.

In late summer each female lays a string of 300 to 400 eggs in a depression under a rock. Sometimes several females deposit in the same nest. The male attends the eggs. They hatch into larvae about 30 mm long. When 100–130 mm in length and 18 months of age, larvae lose their gills, but their many irregular dark spots may persist. Hellbenders eat crayfish, earthworms, and insects. They are often captured by fishermen using live bait but are best collected by overturning rocks in shallow water and using a dip net. Contrary to rumors, Hellbenders are nonpoisonous.

### Dwarf Siren *Pseudobranchus striatus*

100 to 152 mm (4 to 6 in.) These small, slender, eellike salamanders have external gills and tiny forelegs but no hindlegs. Unlike other sirens, the dorsum and sides of the body are brown and conspicuously striped with yellow. The venter is grayish green with many yellow flecks. Dwarf Sirens also have a smaller and slimmer body, a more pointed snout, three digits per limb, and only one pair of gill slits.

These sluggish salamanders inhabit the southern half of the coastal plain in South Carolina. They find food and shelter in mud or amid the aquatic vegetation of a swamp, marsh, ditch, or pond. To collect Dwarf Sirens, seine bottom detritus or gather masses of vegetation and take them ashore for careful sorting.

Dwarf Sirens feed on small, slow-moving, or dead organisms: chironomid larvae, amphipods, ostracods, and worms. During drought, Dwarf Sirens may become encased in dried mud and survive for many months. Under such conditions the gills atrophy but can attain normal size within a week after the return of water.

**Lesser Siren** *Siren intermedia*

150 to 380 mm (6 to 15 in.) This large, slimy, eellike salamander lacks hind limbs but has front limbs (each with four digits) and external gills. The costal grooves total 31 to 35 and average 32.7. The dorsum is black or brown, sometimes with minute black dots; the venter is slightly paler. This species is smaller and more slender than the Greater Siren and has fewer costal grooves.

Lesser Sirens inhabit the coastal plain in the Carolinas. They prefer the quiet weed-choked waters of swamps, ditches, and ponds.

Sirens communicate with one another by a series of click sounds made by rapid snapping of the horny jaws. In early spring a female lays about 200 eggs in a small depression on the bottom of a pond. Hatchlings are 11 mm long. The body and head soon become boldly marked with a middorsal, a lateral, and a ventrolateral light stripe. These stripes turn orange or red only to disappear within a year. The lateral marking on the snout is the most persistent. Also, it is more conspicuous (redder and broader) than that of young Greater Sirens.

### Greater Siren *Siren lacertina*

510 to 950 mm (20 to 37.5 in.) This very large, eellike salamander lacks hind limbs but has small front limbs (each with four digits) and external gills. The dorsum is olive to light gray, sometimes with black spots. The venter is bluish gray with many small greenish yellow flecks or spots. Larger size and more costal grooves (36 to 40) distinguish this species from the Lesser Siren.

Greater Sirens inhabit the coastal plain in most of Virginia and all of the Carolinas. They are nocturnal and favor muddy and weed-choked ditches, swamps, ponds, as well as large lakes and streams.

Greater Sirens eat crustaceans, mollusks, worms, insects, and large amounts of algae. Extensive fat deposits enable sirens to survive several years without feeding, as when stranded by drought in underground chambers or burrows. Each female lays about 500 eggs in small groups scattered about on the bottom. Hatchlings measure 16 mm in total length and during much of the first year of life, have a red or yellow stripe on each side of the body and another on the dorsal fin.

*Eastern Newt (adult)*

*Eastern Newt (eft)*

**Eastern Newt** *Notophthalmus viridescens*

60 to 140 mm (2.5 to 5.5 in.) The aquatic adults are yellowish brown to olive green or darker green above, and yellow with small black spots below. Red spots encircled with black occur on the dorsum

of most populations, but the coastal plain populations from the southern half of North Carolina to the Santee River in South Carolina have broken red stripes with black borders, and those from south of the Santee lack or have reduced dorsal markings. Terrestrial subadults (efts) have thicker, rougher skins, and vary from reddish brown to bright orange red. This species lacks costal grooves.

Adults live in ponds, lakes, and pools near rivers and streams, and efts inhabit moist, forested areas. This species is common to abundant throughout our area.

An elaborate courtship occurs in the spring and fall. The female deposits her eggs singly on leaves of submerged plants in ponds or lakes in late winter, spring, and early summer. She may fold a leaf around each egg, effectively hiding it from view. Hatching occurs after a developmental period of up to 35 days, and the newly emerged larvae average 7.5 mm long. Transformation of the larvae into terrestrial efts takes place in the summer or fall, but in some areas of the coastal plain the eft stage is omitted. Newly transformed young are about 36–41 mm long. The details of the life cycle vary considerably throughout the area and over the entire range. Newts feed on a variety of aquatic invertebrates, including insects, crustaceans, and mollusks. They also eat the eggs of other salamanders and frogs. These animals make excellent aquarium pets.

### Carolina Mudpuppy *Necturus lewisi*

170 to 276 mm (6.5 to 11 in.) Mudpuppies differ from other large salamanders by having four toes on each hind foot and conspicuous gills which are retained throughout life. This species differs from the Common Mudpuppy in having a lighter dorsal color with more pattern contrast and a more heavily spotted venter. Juveniles lack the median dark stripe of that species. Dark spots form gradually in juveniles, first in the dorsal area, and then as maturity approaches, they invade the venter. The head is more depressed and the body is stockier than in the Dwarf Mudpuppy.

This species is endemic to North Carolina. It inhabits the main streams and larger tributaries of the Neuse and Tar rivers from well above tidewater into the lower piedmont. It prefers leaf beds in quiet water in winter; only infrequently is it found in summer.

In April and May, females bear large-yolked eggs; nests have not been described but probably are located under submerged objects. Sexual maturity is attained at an age of about 6 years and some are thought to live 18 years.

**Common Mudpuppy** *Necturus maculosus*

203 to 228 mm (8 to 9 in.) Juveniles of the Common Mudpuppy
have a dark middorsal stripe flanked by pale tan stripes and dark
sides. With growth the striped pattern is replaced by a brown
ground color with scattered dark spots on back, sides, and belly.
Adults attain a much larger size in the north, up to 432 mm.

In our area, this species is known only from the Holston, Clinch,
and French Broad systems, but is thought to occur in the Little
Tennessee River drainage. Common Mudpuppies are most readily
found in late fall or early winter
when they aggregate in leaf beds
in slack water. They eat crayfish,
insect larvae, worms, and other
small aquatic organisms.

Breeding has not been observed
in our area, but farther north, 60
to 80 eggs are laid in June on
the underside of large rocks in
the shallow water of lakes and
streams where hatching occurs in
midsummer.

**Dwarf Mudpuppy** *Necturus punctatus*

115 to 190 mm (4.5 to 7.5 in.) Most Dwarf Mudpuppies are uniformly dark brown above and pale below; however, in the Cape Fear and Lumber systems, most adults are distinctly spotted, especially on the tail. The spots are about the same size as the eye, smaller than in the Carolina Mudpuppy. The Dwarf Mudpuppy is also smaller, more slender, and more cylindrical.

This species occurs from the Chowan River, Virginia, to the Ocmulgee-Altamaha system in Georgia. It inhabits smaller streams than does *N. lewisi*, and is found down to the upper limits of tidewater. Along the fall line in the Tar and Neuse rivers of North Carolina the two species occur together. Juveniles burrow in the silty bottoms of streams. In the winter, adults congregate in leaf beds.

Nests are unknown but small specimens appear in the fall. Maturity is reached a year earlier than in *N. lewisi* and large specimens are probably at least 10 years old.

These animals do well in aquariums provided with leaves or silt in which to burrow and small aquatic arthropods or worms on which to feed.

**Two-toed Amphiuma** *Amphiuma means*

460 to 1162 mm (18 to 46 in.) This robust, eellike salamander
has two pairs of tiny legs with two toes on each foot. The body is
dark brown to black above and dark gray below. The superficially
similar Sirens have bushy, external gills and a pair of anterior legs.

   This relatively common species inhabits streams, abandoned rice fields, and ditches or shallow ponds in pine savannas, hardwood forests, and swamps. It occurs throughout the coastal plain and in portions of the adjacent piedmont.

Two-toed Amphiumas eat insects, crayfish, mollusks, other amphibians, and small reptiles. They can bite viciously; handle them with caution! The life history of this species is poorly known. In winter, females deposit long, rosarylike strings of eggs in depressions beneath logs, boards, or other objects in moist or wet areas. They attend the eggs which hatch about 5 months later into aquatic larvae averaging 55 mm long. Recently transformed young are about 70 mm long.

### Flatwoods Salamander *Ambystoma cingulatum*

90 to 129 mm (3.5 to 5 in.) This dark salamander has grayish reticulations on the dorsum and sides and light flecks on the venter. It differs from other *Ambystoma* by its small size, slender body with a relatively small head, distinct reticulated markings, and 15 costal grooves (rather than 11 to 13). Mabee's Salamander is also small but is dark brown with light lateral flecks.

The Flatwoods Salamander occurs in the southern half of the coastal plain of South Carolina. The chief habitat is flatwoods dominated by pines and wire grass. These uncommon salamanders may be found beneath logs near cypress ponds, swamps, and pitcher plant bogs.

Breeding occurs in November. An average of 150 eggs are laid in small groups on the ground. The eggs are unattended and hatch a few weeks later when the site is flooded by rain. The larvae are very colorful, black with conspicuous light, longitudinal stripes. Metamorphosis occurs in March or April when the length is about 70 mm.

**Jefferson Salamander** *Ambystoma jeffersonianum*

110 to 220 mm (4.25 to 8.5 in.) This dark brown or gray salamander is more slender than most species of *Ambystoma* and has long, slim toes and a laterally compressed tail. It is marked on the sides with bluish flecks, which are most apparent on juveniles. The Slimy Salamander is similar but has a round tail.

Jefferson Salamanders inhabit low woods and bottomlands from New England south mainly in the valley and ridge province of Virginia to the New River.

With the first warm rains of spring they migrate to woodland ponds to court and spawn. The male deposits gelatinous spermatophores on debris in the water, and with her vent the courted female nips off the sperm-bearing cap to provide internal fertilization. Later, along twigs and stems she lays about 10 egg masses, each with 15 to 20 eggs. The larvae hatch in about a month at about 12 mm and transform in midsummer at 50 to 75 mm. First breeding occurs about 18 months later.

### Mabee's Salamander *Ambystoma mabeei*

80 to 114 mm (3 to 4.5 in.) This brown salamander has a relatively small head and long slender toes. Silvery white flecks are abundant along the sides but sparse on the back. The Slimy Salamander is similar but is black and has a nasolabial groove. Mole Salamanders are also brown with light flecking, but are much stockier and have larger, broader heads. Flatwoods Salamanders are dark gray, more slender, and have more dorsal flecks.

Mabee's Salamander is characteristically a pine savanna species, living in burrows at the edges of bogs or ponds. It also occurs in low wet woods and swamps. The range of this species includes most of the coastal plain in the Carolinas.

The breeding season extends from late fall to early spring. It typically follows that of the Flatwoods Salamander. The female attaches her eggs singly or in loose chains of two to six to leaves, twigs, or other bottom debris in shallow ponds. The aquatic larvae hatch after 9 to 14 days and average 8.5 mm long. Transformation occurs in late spring at sizes of 50 to 60 mm.

**Spotted Salamander** *Ambystoma maculatum*

150 to 249 mm (6 to 10 in.) Bright yellow round spots in two irregular rows on a dark background identify this stout-bodied species.
The Tiger Salamander is similar, but its light markings are more
oval and less regular in position. Specimens from the mountains
average 25 mm longer than those from the piedmont.

Spotted Salamanders inhabit deciduous forests with semipermanent pools about 1 m deep. They avoid bottomlands subject
to regular flooding and permanent ponds containing fish. They are
common in the piedmont and mountains, but because of their
fossorial habits, they are rarely found except during the short
breeding season. This species is scattered but locally common on
the coastal plain.

With the first warm rains in
winter to early spring, these salamanders leave their burrows and
migrate by night to the breeding
ponds. Eggs are laid in masses of
up to 200 on sticks and stems in
the water. With the next rain the
adults return to their burrows.
The eggs hatch in 30 to 55 days.
The larvae transform about June,
attain the adult pattern a few days
later, and begin their fossorial life.

**Marbled Salamander** *Ambystoma opacum*

90 to 127 mm (3.5 to 5 in.) This stocky salamander is shiny black with conspicuous white crossbands over the back. These are brighter and more distinct in males, especially during the breeding season. No other salamander in our area has such markings.

Marbled Salamanders occur throughout the area but are uncommon in the mountains. They reside under logs or rocks, usually in swamps or in moist sandy areas along ponds and streams.

Unlike most species in the genus, Marbled Salamanders breed in autumn. They court on land, and each female lays about 100 eggs in a small depression in the soil beneath leaves or a log. The eggs are guarded by the female. They hatch after winter rains inundate the nest sites to form temporary ponds. The larvae transform in April or May. Adults are more readily found throughout the year than are other *Ambystoma*. Marbled Salamanders make interesting pets and are easily maintained in a terrarium provided with damp soil or leaf litter. They eat earthworms, insects, and snails but can be trained to eat small pieces of meat.

**Mole Salamander** *Ambystoma talpoideum*

80 to 122 mm (3 to 5 in.) This gray, brown, or dark brown salamander has a large head, a short stocky body, and relatively large
legs. Scattered bluish white flecks are present on the back and
sides. The belly is bluish gray with light flecks, except in recently
transformed young which have a dark median stripe, a remnant of
the larval pattern.

Mole Salamanders occupy underground burrows in pine
savannas, hardwood forests, and swamps. They are not often
encountered except during the breeding season when they congregate in shallow ponds. The range includes the southern half of
the South Carolina coastal plain and several localities in western
North Carolina.

In the coastal plain, breeding
occurs in winter. Females deposit
10 to 41 eggs in small, loose clusters attached to stems or other objects in shallow ponds. The larvae
transform in the summer and fall
but may overwinter; neoteny
occurs in some populations. The
newly transformed young are 55
to 70 mm long.

**Tiger Salamander** *Ambystoma tigrinum*

178 to 279 mm (7 to 11 in.) This large salamander has yellow or yellowish brown spots against a background of dark brown or black. The irregular spots extend well onto the sides. The belly is yellowish, marbled with darker pigment. Spotted Salamanders are similar but have two distinct rows of yellow spots on the back and yellow or reddish orange spots on the head.

This rare species is known only from widely scattered localities in the coastal plain and from two localities in the piedmont of South Carolina. It inhabits burrows in sandy areas near shallow ponds chiefly in pine savannas. The larvae are occasionally found in rivers.

The life history of this species in the southeastern United States is poorly known. Freshly deposited eggs and gravid females have been found in the winter and early spring. The loose, globular, or oblong egg cluster contains about 50 eggs and is attached to stems in shallow ponds. The larvae transform in the late spring and summer at an average total length of about 120 mm.

*Photograph by R. E. Ashton, Jr.*

## Green Salamander *Aneides aeneus*

80 to 140 mm (3 to 5.5 in.) This dorsoventrally flattened salamander has green or yellowish green lichenlike patches on a background of dark brown or gray. The belly is pale yellowish white. The limbs and tail are relatively long; the toes are webbed and have expanded tips.

Green Salamanders inhabit moist crevices on shaded rock out-crops in hardwood forests. They are occasionally found on trees. In our area, this now scarce species is known only from scattered localities in the mountains of southwest Virginia, southwest North Carolina, and northwest South Carolina.

In late spring or early summer, females deposit clusters of 10 to 26 eggs on the upper walls of crevices. They remain with the eggs throughout the development period of 84 to 91 days. Hatching occurs in the late summer or early fall. The newly hatched young average about 20 mm long and are miniature replicas of the adults. These salamanders hibernate in deep anastomosing crevices from November through late March.

## Cherokee Salamander *Desmognathus aeneus*

44 to 57 mm (1.75 to 2.25 in.) This tiny salamander has a reddish
bronze dorsal band with a median series of dark irregular spots
or a dark line; chevronlike marks are sometimes present. There
is usually a Y-shaped mark on the head and a dorsal, yellowish
or reddish spot on the thigh. The belly is heavily mottled with
dark pigment. Pigmy Salamanders and young Mountain Dusky
Salamanders are similar but generally have unpigmented bellies.
Pigmy Salamanders are also stockier, have a dorsal yellowish or
reddish spot on the upper arm and the thigh, and silvery pigment
on the lower sides of the body.

Cherokee Salamanders live beneath leaf litter near seepages,
springs, or streams in hardwood forests.
In our area, they occur southwest of the Little
Tennessee River in southwestern North
Carolina.

In April or May, females deposit
compact clusters of about 12
eggs beneath moss in seepages or
springs. They remain with the
eggs which hatch in late spring or
early summer. Hatchlings resemble the adults; there is no aquatic
larval stage.

## Southern Dusky Salamander *Desmognathus auriculatus*

80 to 163 mm (3 to 6.5 in.) This dark brown to almost black salamander has two rows of conspicuous white or reddish orange
spots on each side of the body. The laterally compressed tail is
trigonal in cross section at the base, is keeled, and has a middorsal
reddish orange stripe. The belly is dark brown and heavily pep-
pered with white or pale yellow. Some *D. fuscus* are similar, but
have a lighter belly, less conspicuous lateral light spots, and a
more tapered tail. Larvae of the two species are more easily distinguished. The gills of *D. auriculatus* larvae are bushy, pigmented,
and have 30 to 43 filaments on each side; those of *D. fuscus* are less
bushy, glistening white, and have 19 to 33 filaments on each side.

 *D. auriculatus* is abundant
under leaf litter and rotten logs in
swamps and bottomland forests
throughout the coastal plain.

 In summer, females deposit
clusters of 9 to 20 eggs in cavities
beneath moss or within rotten logs
near water. They remain with the
eggs until they hatch into aquatic
larvae in the early fall. Transformation occurs in late spring.

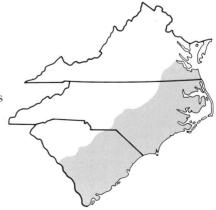

**Northern Dusky Salamander** *Desmognathus fuscus*

60 to 141 mm (2.5 to 5.5 in.) The young of this highly variable salamander usually have five to eight pairs of buff-colored, yellow, or reddish orange dorsal spots on a background of dark brown or gray. Many older individuals have a wide dorsal band with dark wavy or scalloped edges extending to the base of the tail. Others may be uniformly dark gray or brown. The belly is usually mottled lightly with gray or brown. The tail is keeled and compressed. The Mountain Dusky Salamander has a round tail which tapers to a filament. See also the account of the Southern Dusky Salamander.

Northern Dusky Salamanders are abundant in streams, springs, and seepages in bottomland forests and wooded ravines in the piedmont, portions of the upper coastal plain, and some mountain areas.

In summer, females deposit compact clusters of about 23 eggs in cavities of rotten logs, in stream banks or seepages, or on the undersurfaces of rocks in streams. They remain with the eggs until they hatch into aquatic larvae in the late summer or fall. Transformation occurs late in the following spring.

*Photograph by Stephen G. Tilley*

*Photograph by Stephen G. Tilley*

**Imitator Salamander** *Desmognathus imitator*

70 to 110 mm (3 to 4.5 in.) This cryptic species resembles *D. och-rophaeus* in size and general appearance but differs in genetic makeup. Many populations of *D. imitator* vary markedly in color

and pattern and can be distinguished from *D. ochrophaeus* only by electrophoretic analysis. At present, only certain populations along the main ridge of the Great Smoky Mountains can be distinguished from *D. ochrophaeus* by their color patterns. Most *D. imitator* from these populations have strongly undulating dorsal stripes bordering an indistinct dorsal band. In contrast, most *D. ochrophaeus* have a distinct dorsal band of light yellow to dark brown bordered along each side by a straight to moderately undulating black stripe. Many individuals of both species darken with age and become almost black and patternless. All *D. ochrophaeus* from the Smokies lack colored cheek patches, but many *D. imitator* have colored cheeks and mimic closely the red-cheeked Jordan's Salamander. To distinguish *D. imitator* from *Plethodon jordani*, look for these desmognathine features: (1) a trace of a lightish area immediately behind the eye, (2) a bent-head profile, and (3) hindlegs much larger than forelegs.

Imitator Salamanders are endemic to the Great Smoky National Park area. They occur under rocks, logs, and leaf litter in cool, moist spruce-fir and hardwood forests. *D. imitator* is broadly sympatric with *D. ochrophaeus*, but in the Great Smokies the latter is more restricted to the higher elevations. *D. imitator* is also less terrestrial and prefers the environs of intermittent streams; *D. ochrophaeus* can be found on the forest floor, sometimes far from water.

Information on life history must await further study.

**Seal Salamander** *Desmognathus monticola*

80 to 149 mm (3 to 6 in.) This robust, buff-colored, greenish gray, or light brown salamander has dark wavy or wormlike marks on its back, and a pale or lightly mottled belly. The posterior half of the tail is keeled and laterally compressed. The young are green with four pairs of reddish orange spots. In the Virginia Blue Ridge, the dark dorsal markings are usually reduced to scattered, round dots. Northern Dusky Salamanders are smaller, less robust, and have more heavily mottled bellies and shorter tails.

Seal Salamanders are abundant at the edges of streams, seepages, and springs. They occur throughout the mountains and in adjacent portions of the piedmont.

In early summer, females deposit clusters of 16 to 39 eggs in cavities in rotten logs or stream banks, or on the undersurfaces of rocks in streams. They remain with the eggs until they hatch into aquatic larvae in late summer or early fall. Transformation occurs after a few weeks at lengths of 23 to 30 mm.

**Mountain Dusky Salamander** *Desmognathus ochrophaeus*

70 to 111 mm (3 to 4.5 in.) Amazing variation in color, markings, body proportions, and size characterize these alert salamanders. The variation is individual, ontogenetic, and geographic. Males average 12 percent longer than the females. Most young animals are dorsally spotted, but many adults are drab and nondescript,

while others have gay patterns and bright colors. Most specimens from northern Virginia have a straight-edged, light dorsal band, but more southern specimens have an uneven and more variable dorsal band. Red-cheeked specimens do not inhabit the Smokies, but are occasional in the Nantahalas, and Highlands plateau. (See account of *D. imitator*.) Red-legged ones are restricted to the southern Nantahalas. In contrast, individuals from Mount Mitchell are very large and dark, with short tails and small heads. This species is similar to the Northern Dusky Salamander but is more terrestrial, often more brightly colored, and more variably marked. The tail is longer, rounder, and more tapered and usually lacks a dorsal keel. The males also have a darker body and a more curved jaw margin than the females.

Mountain Dusky Salamanders occur throughout most of the mountains but are uncommon at low elevations. At low elevations they inhabit seepages and stream margins, but at high elevations they range away from streams and appear under rocks, leaves, and logs in woodlands.

Most spawn in July but a few spawn in March. The average clutch contains 15 eggs (5 to 40, depending on the size of the female). The eggs are laid in crevices through which water trickles or under moss alongside seepages. Often the egg clutches are a few inches apart, but each is attended by the female. The eggs hatch in about 6 weeks, and the hatchlings are 8 to 10 mm from snout to vent. Metamorphosis takes place in 2 to 8 months.

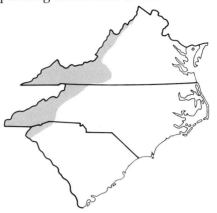

**Blackbelly Salamander** *Desmognathus quadramaculatus*

100 to 210 mm (4 to 8 in.) This large, robust salamander has a brown or dark greenish gray back, a black belly, and a short, keeled tail. Two rows of conspicuous white spots are usually visible on each side of the trunk. In young subadults the belly is unpigmented; older subadults have patches of black interspersed with areas of yellowish white. Although a dark Shovelnose Salamander is similar, it lacks the sharp contrast in color between the belly and the lower sides and has a flattened, wedge-shaped snout and smaller eyes.

Blackbelly Salamanders inhabit mountain streams and often rest on wet rock ledges near waterfalls, seepages, or springs. They occur in the mountains throughout the Carolinas and southwestern Virginia and in portions of the adjacent piedmont.

In summer, a female deposits a cluster of 21 to 62 eggs on the undersurface of a rock or on tree roots in a streambed. She remains with the eggs until they hatch into aquatic larvae in late summer or early fall. The larval period lasts about 24 months.

**Cumberland Salamander** *Desmognathus welteri*

80 to 170 mm (3 to 6.5 in.) This large nondescript salamander is brown, usually with scattered dark spots, but occasional specimens are uniformly tan above. The venter is yellow and lightly mottled with dark pigment, and the toes are dark-tipped. Sympatric Northern Dusky Salamanders have dorsolateral dark stripes and light toe tips, and Seal Salamanders have a dorsal pattern of heavier brown spots or bars, remnants of the rims of the juvenile spots, and pale and evenly pigmented bellies. The Cumberland Salamander is also more aquatic and its larval stage lasts nearly 2 years, whereas that of the Northern Dusky and the Seal Salamander is less than a year.

This recently described species is known from the Cumberland Mountain area of southeastern Kentucky and southwestern Virginia. Adults prefer large turbulent brooks, living under stones and in crevices in the splash zone. Larvae and juveniles inhabit spring seep tributaries.

About 26 eggs per clutch are laid in the spring and summer months. The female usually coils about the eggs as she attends them.

## Pigmy Salamander *Desmognathus wrighti*

38 to 51 mm (1.5 to 2 in.) This diminutive salamander usually has a reddish bronze dorsal band with a median series of chevronlike marks, silvery pigment on the lower sides of the body, an unpigmented belly, and a short tail. The snout and eyelids are moderately to conspicuously rugose. The similar Cherokee Salamander has a pigmented belly, a median dark stripe or series of dots, and a longer tail; the snout and eyelids are usually smooth. Chevrons, if present, do not extend the width of the dorsal band.

Pigmy Salamanders live under moss, leaf litter, rotten logs, bark on stumps, or rocks in spruce-fir forests, but move into seepage areas in winter. Some populations occur in hardwood forests at lower elevations. This species is endemic to the high mountains of southwestern Virginia, western North Carolina, and adjacent Tennessee.

This species is active chiefly on dark, humid nights, and may climb trees to heights of about 2 m. In late summer, a female deposits a cluster of about 10 eggs in an underground cavity near a seepage or stream. The hatchlings have conspicuous spots, but otherwise resemble adults.

## Two-lined Salamander *Eurycea bislineata*

64 to 121 mm (2.5 to 5 in.) This slender salamander has a yellow to reddish orange dorsal band with black dots or flecks. A dark dorsolateral stripe extends to at least mid-tail. In the northern half of Virginia and throughout the mountains, the posterior half of the tail stripe is usually broken into spots. Elsewhere, the stripe usually extends to the tip of the tail. The belly is yellow to reddish orange. Breeding males have a slender cirrus extending downward from each nostril. Dwarf Salamanders are similar, but have only four toes on each hind foot; Two-lined Salamanders have five.

Two-lined Salamanders live in or near springs, seepages, and streams in hardwood forests and swamps. They occur throughout the area, but are most numerous in the mountains.

Courtship occurs in the fall, and the eggs are laid in the winter and spring. The female deposits a flat cluster of eggs on the under-surfaces of a rock or log, usually in running water. She remains with the eggs until they hatch into aquatic larvae.

## Three-lined Salamander *Eurycea guttolineata*

90 to 200 mm (3.5 to 8 in.) This species resembles the Longtail Salamander in size and shape. A black median stripe is flanked by a pair of tan stripes, which meet on the base of the tail; the sides are dark with a light streak between the limbs, and the venter is tan and marbled with dark pigment.

The Three-lined Salamander occurs commonly in creek bottomlands in the piedmont, is locally common in the coastal plain, and is restricted to larger valleys in the mountains. It hybridizes with the Longtail Salamander along a narrow band across northern Georgia, Alabama, and Mississippi. In our area the two species are distinct, but they seldom occur together.

Freshly laid eggs have not been described, but hatching eggs and larvae less than 20 mm were found in mid-March in western North Carolina. The young transform in 4 or 5 months and then live under logs, stones, and debris along stream bottomlands. Sexual maturity is reached the following summer, and breeding presumably takes place in the autumn or winter.

## Junaluska Salamander *Eurycea junaluska*

80 to 100 mm (3 to 4 in.) The dull yellow brown dorsum is sprinkled with small melanophores. A wavy, broken black stripe extends from the nostril through the eye and along the side of the body. On the tail it becomes a series of small dots or thin lines. The venter is light greenish yellow. This species has 14 costal grooves. The tail is about half the total length. Males have a well-developed mental gland but lack cirri. The Junaluska Salamander resembles the sympatric Two-lined Salamander but has longer legs, a shorter tail, and intense mottling on the side of the body. Also, the Two-lined Salamander has a broader dorsolateral stripe and a more yellow or orange dorsum.

The Junaluska Salamander is known only from Graham County, North Carolina, and the western tip of the Great Smoky Mountains Park. Although it lives at low altitudes under rocks and logs along streams, most specimens have been collected on roads on rainy nights.

Information on the life history of this recently described species is scant. Metamorphosing individuals are 70 to 85 mm long.

## Longtail Salamander *Eurycea longicauda*

90 to 197 mm (3.5 to 8 in.) This is a slender yellow to orange red species with abundant round black spots on the sides and back and vertical dark bars on the sides of the tail. The belly is unmarked. The tail may be nearly two-thirds of the total length in large adults, but is proportionately shorter in young animals.

In Virginia it is found west of the Blue Ridge, but in North Carolina it is known only from the Watauga, Nantahala, and Little Tennessee river basins. Over most of its range it is usually associated with limestone and shale substrates, and is found along rocky streams and bottomlands, and commonly in damp caves.

Eggs average about 90 per complement and are laid underground. In mines and caves the eggs are attached to stones or boards in or suspended above the water. Larvae hatch in winter at less than 20 mm in length and transformation occurs by early summer at 40–50 mm. Sexual maturity is attained the next summer.

## Cave Salamander *Eurycea lucifuga*

125 to 181 mm (5 to 7 in.) The Cave Salamander is reddish orange
with round black spots scattered over the sides and back, sometimes in irregular rows. The young are paler and yellowish. It is
slender and flattened and has a very long tail. This species differs
from the Longtail Salamander by lacking vertical dark bars on the
sides of the tail and by having a broader head with bulging eyes.

Cave Salamanders occur from Rockbridge County, Virginia,
south and west across the Cumberland plateau to the Ozarks.
Virtually restricted to limestone regions, this species is partial to
the twilight zone of caves and climbs well on damp walls and
ledges, but is not a true troglobite. During wet periods it may occur
near springs and along rocky brooks under logs and stones.

Courtship has not been observed. In the fall or winter a
female attaches about 60 eggs to
the underside of a rock in a cave
stream. Hatchlings are sparsely
pigmented and only 10 mm long.
Metamorphosis occurs at 50 to 60
mm. The young become sexually
mature at about 125 mm. The
duration of each life cycle stage
is unknown.

**Dwarf Salamander** *Eurycea quadridigitata*

54 to 90 mm (2 to 3.5 in.) This small, slender species resembles the Two-lined Salamander but has only four toes on each hind foot; the Two-lined Salamander has five. In some populations, the back is light brownish yellow or bronze and the belly is bright yellow. In others the back is dark brown, the sides have narrow whitish streaks, and the belly is silver gray.

Dwarf Salamanders live beneath leaf litter or rotten logs in bottomland forests, swamps, and at the edges of pine savanna ponds. In the Carolinas, they occur throughout most of the coastal plain and in portions of the piedmont.

In the late fall or winter, females deposit about 22 eggs in seepage areas or near the edges of shallow ponds. The eggs are attached singly to sphagnum strands, pine needles, or leaves, and sometimes to rootlets in cavities beneath logs; they are not attended by the female. Embryonic development requires about 1 month. The aquatic larvae transform in late spring or early summer.

**Spring Salamander** *Gyrinophilus porphyriticus*

120 to 220 mm (4.5 to 8.5 in.) This rather large salamander has a stout body, a broadly truncate snout, and 18 costal grooves. The dorsum is light brownish orange or salmon, often with small dark spots or flecks. A light line, bordered below by a dark line, extends from eye to nostril. The venter is flesh-colored, and the throat may be flecked or reticulated with black. Spring Salamanders resemble *Pseudotriton* but are more agile and have a broader and flatter snout.

Spring Salamanders inhabit springs and other small, cold, rocky streams, and caves in the mountains and the upper piedmont of Virginia and the Carolinas. By day they hide under stones near the edge of streams. Salamanders, large insects, and worms are the dietary staples.

In July or August each female attaches 20 to 60 eggs to the lower surface of a submerged rock. They are attended by the female and hatch in about 3 months. Hatchlings average 25 mm in length. The larvae have a purplish ground color that may persist for about 3 years. Females are about 5 years old at first reproduction.

## Four-toed Salamander *Hemidactylium scutatum*

50 to 95 mm (2 to 3.5 in.) This small brown salamander has a white belly with conspicuous scattered black dots, a reddish tail constricted at the base where it breaks easily, and four toes on each hind foot.

Though this species is widely distributed in the northeastern United States, its populations are scattered in our area. This bog dweller requires seepages or shallow ponds with moss-covered logs, roots, and grass clumps over quiet water. In the coastal plain of the Carolinas, the Four-toed Salamander is known from only a few localities.

The female lays about 30 to 50 eggs under moss and attends them until hatching. Large aggregations of eggs, the efforts of several females, often occur. In our area spawning occurs in about early March, hatching May. The larvae, about 12 mm long, wriggle down into the water for a growth period of about 6 weeks. At about 20 mm in length they emerge as terrestrial juveniles and mature 1 ½ years later.

**Shovelnose Salamander** *Leurognathus marmoratus*

88 to 143 mm (3.5 to 5.5 in.) The dorsum is usually dark brown with two rows of light blotches. Typically, a light area extends from eye to angle of jaw, as occurs in species of *Desmognathus*. The venter is usually dark gray with a whitish central area. Specimens from the Nantahala River drainage are especially dark. An interesting type of depigmentation occurs especially in southern populations. These individuals are mostly whitish yellow but may have dark blotches. *Leurognathus* is often confused with the Blackbelly Salamander but is more aquatic and has a broader tail fin, a flatter snout, and slitlike internal nostrils.

*Leurognathus* inhabit trout streams in the mountains from southwestern Virginia to northeastern Georgia. They spend much time under rocks and feed mainly on aquatic insects.

Spawning occurs chiefly in June. Eggs average 40 per clutch and are attached to the underside of a rock in the main current. The female stays with her eggs throughout the 2½ months of development. Hatchlings are 20 mm in length; they metamorphose 10 to 20 months later when 40 to 65 mm long.

### Redback Salamander *Plethodon cinereus*

57 to 127 mm (2.25 to 5 in.) This small salamander usually has a straight-edged reddish dorsal stripe and a heavily mottled black and white belly. Unstriped uniformly dark gray or black individuals with scattered brassy or white (occasionally reddish) flecks occur in some populations. Red pigment on the anterior belly, often present in *P. serratus*, is usually absent. *P. dorsalis* has a dorsal stripe with zigzag edges, at least anteriorly, and reddish orange pigment over the entire belly. *P. richmondi* and *P. hubrichti* are more slender and have longer tails and distinctly darker bellies.

Redback Salamanders live under rocks, leaf litter, and rotten logs in forests. They occur in the mountains north and east of the French Broad River and in portions of the piedmont and coastal plain.

The mating period extends from October to April. In June the female deposits a cluster of 8 to 10 eggs usually within a cavity in a well-rotted log. She attends the eggs until they hatch in late August or September into terrestrial young.

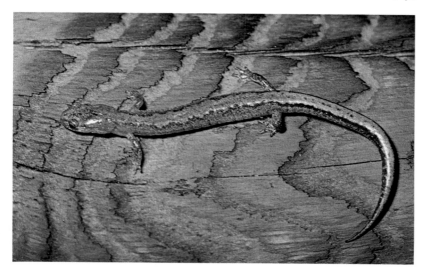

## Zigzag Salamander *Plethodon dorsalis*

64 to 111 mm (2.5 to 4.5 in.) This small salamander has a reddish orange to reddish brown dorsal band with wavy or zigzag edges at least on its anterior half. The belly is heavily mottled with black, white, and reddish orange. The two Redback Salamanders have straight-edged reddish dorsal bands. If ventral reddish orange pigment is present, it is confined to the area between the front limbs.

Zigzag Salamanders are usually associated with seepages near rock outcrops on slopes in mixed hardwood forests, and live under leaf litter, rocks, or rotten logs. This very rare species is known in our area only from Henderson County, North Carolina.

Little is known about the life history of this salamander in our area. Most surface activity occurs in the spring; individuals become increasingly scarce and are difficult to find at other times. The known populations are possibly relicts of a widespread Pleistocene population.

### Slimy Salamander *Plethodon glutinosus*

120 to 206 mm (4.5 to 8 in.) The Slimy Salamander is black with white or cream flecks scattered over the sides or, sometimes, on the back and limbs. Some populations in the coastal plain lack the white pigment altogether, and in others it is concentrated into lateral bands. Glands in the skin, especially on the tail, exude a sticky slime that is difficult to remove from the hands.

This ubiquitous salamander probably occurs in woodlands in every part of our area, except bottomlands subject to repeated flooding, some of the higher mountain slopes, and the Delmarva Peninsula. Slimy Salamanders are active near the surface from spring to fall except during dry periods when they move underground. They forage at night and spend the day in burrows under logs, stones, and leaf litter.

Eggs are laid in or under logs and among roots, but are rarely found. In the coastal plain, each female lays her eggs annually in late summer or fall, but in the mountains only every other spring.

**Valley and Ridge Salamander** *Plethodon hoffmani*

80 to 137 mm (3 to 5.5 in.) This slender salamander has short legs,
a long tail, and usually 21 costal grooves. The dorsum is dark
brown to blackish with scattered whitish or brassy flecks. The
venter is dark with white mottling, especially on the chin. Most
specimens from along the West Virginia border have but 20 costal
grooves and some have a narrow dorsal red stripe. *P. hoffmani* has
1 or 2 more costal grooves than the similarly proportioned *P. hubrichti* and *P. richmondi*. In addition, the chin and belly are lighter
in *P. hubrichti*, but are darker in *P. richmondi*.

This salamander lives under logs and rocks in the ridge and
valley physiographic province north of the New River in Virginia.

Life history data are scant.
These salamanders tolerate cool
weather well; they appear early
in March and disappear in late
summer, but are active during
the early half of fall. Females attend their eggs until hatching
and the young mature in 2 years.
Like most salamanders, they eat
invertebrates.

## Peaks of Otter Salamander *Plethodon hubrichti*

80 to 122 mm (3 to 5 in.) The dorsum is black with numerous brassy flecks often forming small spots or blotches. A narrow reddish dorsal stripe is found only in hatchlings, although some older individuals may have a roughly continuous coppery stripe. The venter is black or dark slate gray. A few small white spots occur on the cheeks and sides of the body. This species usually has 19 costal grooves. As in most plethodons, the tail is slender and nearly circular in cross section. Males have a large mental gland. The abundant brassy flecks on the dorsum make identification easy. Weller's Salamander also has metallic dorsal markings but it is smaller and has only 16 costal grooves.

The Peaks of Otter Salamander occurs only in cool, moist woods on the Peaks of Otter in Bedford County, Virginia. Individuals reside under logs and rocks and eat most small invertebrates.

A cluster of about 10 eggs is laid in or under a decaying log in May or June. More information on life history and distribution is needed.

**Jordan's Salamander** *Plethodon jordani*

90 to 184 mm (3.5 to 7 in.) This abundant salamander is basically black or dark gray. It resembles an unspotted Slimy Salamander and the relationships of these two species are geographically and genetically complex. In some areas they occur together without hybridizing; in others they produce hybrid swarms. At certain

higher elevations, usually above about 760 m, Jordan's Salamander replaces the Slimy Salamander. Jordan's Salamander has several local color varieties that some herpetologists recognize as subspecies. In the Smoky Mountains, these salamanders have bright orange or red cheeks and are the original *"jordani."* The population in the Nantahala and Tusquitee mountains is the red-legged *"shermani."* The populations east of the Little Tennessee River lack red markings: those south of the Blue Ridge divide and the Swannanoa River are the dark-bellied *"melaventris,"* and those to the north are the smaller and light-bellied *"metcalfi."* A population with silvery dorsal patches, occurring in a small area of northwestern South Carolina, has been called *"clemsonae."* Small juveniles of *"jordani"* and *"shermani"* have reddish dorsal spots, whereas *"melaventris"* and *"metcalfi"* populations lack red pigment. The Slimy Salamander hybridizes with *"jordani," "shermani,"* and the southern and western populations of *"melaventris"* but not with the eastern populations of *"melaventris"* and those of *"metcalfi."* Some *Desmognathus imitator* and *D. ochrophaeus* closely resemble the many local populations of Jordan's Salamander by having red cheeks, red legs, and dark adult color, but these mimics can be recognized by the light bar between the eye and the jaw joint and by the shape of the head.

Like most large *Plethodon*, this species inhabits the forest floor and is active on the surface at night when the humidity is high and the temperature is mild. During the day, it occupies burrows under stones and logs or tunnels formed by rotted roots.

Little is known of the reproductive habits, but the smallest juveniles appear in the spring, indicating fall nesting, probably in underground tunnels.

**Cow Knob Salamander** *Plethodon punctatus*

100 to 157 mm (4 to 6 in.) This blackish salamander is a sibling species of *P. glutinosus*. It has many small white or yellowish white spots on the dorsum and a few brassy flecks on the head and tail. The throat is light, but the remainder of the venter is dark. There are 17 or 18 costal grooves. This species is similar to Wehrle's Salamander but has more webbing between the toes and different dorsal markings: larger and more numerous white spots, fewer brassy flecks, and no red spots on juveniles.

The range is restricted to North Mountain and Shenandoah Mountain in Virginia (near West Virginia). These woodland dwellers occur at elevations above 810 m.

By day they hide under rocks and logs or in burrows, but at night they forage in the open for insects, earthworms, snails, and spiders. Little is known about their life history. They emerge from hibernation in April, are abundant in summer, and retreat to deep burrows by late October. The young mature in 3 years.

**Ravine Salamander** *Plethodon richmondi*

76 to 143 mm (3 to 5.5 in.) This long slender salamander lacks conspicuous markings. The small legs are far apart, separated by 19 to 22 costal grooves. The dorsum is dark brown or almost black with scattered silvery or brassy flecks. The venter is uniformly dark except for some light blotches on the throat and lower sides of the body. Little individual and geographic variation occurs; however, some specimens have red pigment on the cheeks, front legs, and anterior sides of the body. A narrow red dorsal stripe exists only in late embryos. This species differs from the other small *Plethodon* by having more costal grooves and a darker belly and throat.

This salamander inhabits southwestern Virginia and northwestern North Carolina. It prefers high, moist woodlands. Individuals are hard to find during dry summers, but in spring and fall large numbers occur under thin, flat rocks on or partly in the ground.

The life history is poorly known. The two to four hatchlings from each clutch of eggs lack gills and are about 25 mm long.

**Southern Redback Salamander** *Plethodon serratus*

57 to 127 mm (2.25 to 5 in.) This cryptic species is very similar to
*P. cinereus* but differs in biochemical characteristics determined by
electrophoretic analysis of proteins. Few external differences exist,
and those that do are not diagnostic. An unstriped dorsal pattern,
though rare in *P. serratus*, has some dorsal red pigment; that of
*P. cinereus* usually does not. Red pigment is usually present on the
anterior part of the belly in *P. serratus* but not in *P. cinereus*.

   *P. serratus* and *P. cinereus* live in similar habitats, but in our area
they are geographically isolated. *P. serratus* occurs in the mountains
south and west of the French
Broad River. It has not been reported in South Carolina.

   The life history of this species
is presumably similar to that of
*P. cinereus*. Both are cool-weather
forms, moving into deeper underground retreats in the late spring
and summer. Small arthropods
and mollusks constitute the chief
foods.

## Shenandoah Salamander *Plethodon shenandoah*

76 to 110 mm (3 to 4.5 in.) This small dark salamander has two color phases. Some individuals have a narrow red or yellow stripe on the back and others have only scattered brassy flecks and small red spots. Striped individuals constitute about 50 percent of southern populations and 100 percent of northern ones. The venter is black with only a few small white or yellow spots. The costal grooves average 18 per individual. *P. cinereus* is similar but has an average of 19 costal grooves, a broader and darker dorsal stripe, a lighter and more mottled venter, and a narrower head. *P. richmondi* also has more costal grooves but lacks a striped phase and has a plain black venter.

*P. shenandoah* occurs only on the highest mountains in the Shenandoah National Park in northern Virginia. It is surprisingly tolerant of dry conditions found on steep, north-facing talus slopes.

**Webster's Salamander** *Plethodon websteri*

60 to 110 mm (2.5 to 4.5 in.) This recently described species closely resembles *P. dorsalis* and must be identified biochemically; there are no reliable external characteristics. However, the zigzag pattern is absent or confined to the dorsal band's anterior third or half. The dorsum varies from bright to dusky reddish orange, brightest on the tail which typically has less dark pigment than the body. The venter is mottled with black, white, and reddish orange, with the orange especially prominent on the neck. Specimens from our area differ from those in other parts of the range by having a mode of 19 rather than 18 costal grooves.

Webster's Salamander is known to occur from McCormick County, South Carolina westward into Mississippi, generally south of the range of the Zigzag Salamander. It inhabits moist, mixed hardwood forest on steep north-facing slopes with rock outcrops.

The life history of this species is unknown. However, like *P. dorsalis* it is active mainly in the spring. During the warmer, drier months, individuals move into under-ground retreats.

**Wehrle's Salamander** *Plethodon wehrlei*

100 to 160 mm (4 to 6.5 in.) This species usually is dark gray or
brown with an irregular row of white, bluish white, or yellow
markings on the sides of the body. The venter is uniformly gray
except for white blotches on the throat. Juveniles have red dorsal
spots. Cave populations are highly variable in color and pattern;
e.g., individuals from near Roanoke, Virginia, are purplish brown
with numerous light flecks and bronze mottling. The costal
grooves range from 16 to 18 and average 17. This species resembles the Slimy Salamander but is more slender and has more costal
grooves.

Wehrle's Salamander occupies upland forests in western Virginia and in Stokes County, North Carolina. They inhabit the
entrances of caves and deep rock
crevices, as well as burrows under
rocks and logs on wooded hillsides.

A small cluster of eggs is laid in
early summer in damp logs, soil,
or moss, and in crevices in caves.
Metamorphosis occurs about the
time of hatching. There is no
aquatic larval stage.

### Weller's Salamander *Plethodon welleri*

64 to 79 mm (2.5 to 3 in.) This small black salamander is profusely flecked with brass or gold. The flecks are often fused, forming large, irregular blotches or spots. The belly is usually mottled with white, but is uniformly darker on specimens from Grandfather Mountain, North Carolina.

Weller's Salamanders occur chiefly in spruce-fir forests above 1,500 m. During the day, they hide under rocks, leaf litter, and rotten logs. Populations tend to be associated with talus slopes or other rocky substrates. The range of this species includes mountain areas of southwest Virginia, northwest North Carolina, and northeast Tennessee.

Courtship and mating occur in the spring and fall. At high elevations the female deposits a small cluster of 4 to 11 eggs beneath a mat of moss on a rotten conifer log, probably in early or midsummer. She remains with the eggs until they hatch in late August or early September. The young are miniature replicas of the adults. This salamander feeds primarily on spiders, mites, and insects.

**Yonahlossee Salamander** *Plethodon yonahlossee*

110 to 190 mm (4.5 to 7.5 in.) This large handsome salamander is readily recognized in life by the brick red back and the profuse gray or white spotting on the lower sides. Individuals from southern populations often have red reduced to flecks or blotches on the dorsum. The red colors fade rapidly in preserved specimens which then resemble the Slimy Salamander except for their lighter, more mottled throats.

The Yonahlossee Salamander occurs from mountain valleys to 1,700 m on the mountains of the southern Blue Ridge of Virginia through eastern Tennessee and North Carolina east of the French Broad Valley. It inhabits hillsides and ravines, often where rock slides are thickly carpeted with mosses and ferns. Though locally common, it is more restricted in habitat than most large plethodons.

The reproductive biology is unknown. Stomach analyses indicate a varied diet of arthropods and mollusks. The common ánd specific name of Indian origin derives from the Yonahlossee Road northeast of Linville, North Carolina, whence this species was first described.

## Mud Salamander *Pseudotriton montanus*

73 to 195 mm (3 to 7.5 in.) This robust salamander has a short tail,
brown eyes, and 17 costal grooves. The dorsum is coral pink,
bright red, brownish, or light yellowish orange; the lower sides
are red or yellow. The dorsal spots are small, round, black, and
well separated. Older adults are darker; the dorsum is reddish to
brown with obscure spots and the venter is flecked or mottled with
brown. The Red Salamander has yellow eyes and a larger snout.

Mud Salamanders inhabit the coastal plain and piedmont and
some lowlands in the mountains. They occur in the fine, black
muck beneath logs and stones or in burrows along the banks of
seepages, springs, brooks, or
swamps.

Courtship occurs in early fall,
spawning in December, and
hatching in February. The average
female lays about 127 eggs (66 to
192) every other year. Most larvae
transform in 17 months, but some
require an additional year. The
average snout to vent length is 10
mm at hatching and 36 mm at
metamorphosis. Males mature in
3 years, females in 4 years.

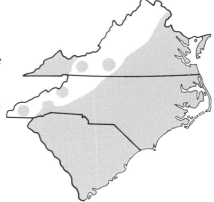

## Red Salamander *Pseudotriton ruber*

76 to 180 mm (3 to 7 in.) This handsome salamander has a short tail and usually 16 costal grooves. The dorsum of young adults is bright red or orange with many black spots, and the belly is salmon red with dark dots. A row of black flecks may border the mouth. Older animals are dark orange or purplish brown with enlarged, fused dorsal spots and more ventral ones. Yellow eyes and a longer snout distinguish the Red from the Mud Salamander.

This species inhabits much of the area, but in the coastal plain of the Carolinas, it is known only from the sandhills and from several counties along the Savannah River. Adults live in leaf accumulations in spring-fed brooks and nearby crevices and burrows. They also live under logs, boards, stones, and leaves in more terrestrial habitats. Earthworms, insects, and small salamanders are their chief food.

Courtship occurs in summer, spawning in October, and hatching in early December. An average clutch contains about 70 eggs. The larval period lasts about 32 months, and the average newly metamorphosed animal is 70 mm long.

## Many-lined Salamander *Stereochilus marginatus*

64 to 114 mm (2.5 to 4.5 in.) This yellowish brown salamander has light and dark streaks or lines on its lower sides. The usually unmarked back sometimes bears a few small, indistinct dark or light spots. The belly is pale dusky yellow with scattered brown flecks. The head is small, narrow, and flattened. The relatively short tail is keeled and laterally compressed.

Many-lined Salamanders inhabit swamps and shallow cypress or gum ponds in pine savannas. They are aquatic but in dry weather adults hide under leaf litter, sphagnum mats, or rotten logs. The range of this species extends north in the coastal plain to eastern Virginia.

In midwinter, the female deposits a cluster of about 60 eggs on an aquatic moss, a twig, or the undersurface of a submerged log. She usually remains with the eggs until they hatch in the early spring. The aquatic larvae transform in the late spring and summer, typically after a larval period of more than 2 years.

# Order Salientia = Anura

FROGS AND TOADS

This large and widely distributed group includes about 2,300 species. Some are aquatic, others arboreal. Many are highly terrestrial, and a few even inhabit regions generally thought of as too harsh for amphibians: deserts, brackish water, and the Arctic. Adults have many unique anatomical features: a stocky body with an extremely short backbone (only 9 or 10 vertebrae), a broad head usually with large eyes, no tail, very long hip bones, and long hind legs. In our area, the adults range in size from 13 mm (Little Grass Frog) to 200 mm (Bullfrog). There are no concise differences between frogs and toads. In general, the term *toad* pertains to the shorter-legged species and customarily includes the bufonids, pelobatids, and microhylids (see species list).

Other important features of most anurans include: lungs, keen hearing, and a well-developed vocal apparatus. Vocalization is especially important during the breeding season when myriads of individuals assemble in rain puddles and ponds. There, the persistent calls of the male play a major role in bringing the sexes of each species together. Hedonic glands are absent. The male clasps the female's groin or axillary region and fertilizes the eggs as they are extruded from her cloaca. All of our species lay their eggs in fresh water. The eggs develop into bizarre larvae popularly known as tadpoles. Tadpoles have many distinct features: large head-trunk region, long muscular tail, cryptic gills, horny beak, and no true teeth. Metamorphosis is obligatory and marked by drastic morphological changes. Overt 'paedomorphosis (retention of larval features), as sometimes occurs in the Caudata, is lacking.

Of the 31 species of Salientia known from the Carolinas and Virginia, most are hylids: 8 *Hyla*, 5 *Pseudacris*, 2 *Acris*, and 1 *Limnaoedus*. The only other large groups are the ranids (true frogs) with 9 species all in the genus *Rana* and the bufonids with 4 species of *Bufo*. *Hyla*, *Rana*, and *Bufo* are nearly cosmopolitan genera, but all of our other genera are restricted to North America. None of our species is endemic but 3 have over two-thirds of their geographic ranges in the Carolinas and Virginia. In contrast to the Caudata, which include many montane species, the Salientia predominately inhabit the coastal plain, especially in the Carolinas.

### Eastern Spadefoot Toad *Scaphiopus holbrooki*

45 to 72 mm (2 to 3 in.) This soft-bodied toad has a distinct tympanum, a small round parotoid gland, and short legs that are often held close to the body. Small tubercles are scattered over the moist skin; it produces a peculiar musty, peppery secretion. The dorsum is usually brown but may be gray or black. A light band extends over the back from eye to vent and another along the side of the body. These bands are more yellowish in males than in females. The throat and chest are white, and the lower belly is light gray or reddish. A pair of large pectoral glands opens onto the chest. The large, protruding eye has a vertical pupil. A spadelike black horny projection is located on the inner border of the foot. This effective digging tool enables a squatting toad to vanish below the surface of loose soil while making only a slight rocking motion with the hind legs. During dry seasons, Spadefoots may remain torpid underground for several weeks. They can survive an enormous loss of water (over 40 percent of body weight).

Being subterranean and nocturnal, Spadefoots are cryptic animals, but they may be found in large numbers when rainfall is extensive. Spadefoots prefer sandy lowlands and are abundant in the coastal plain and the adjacent piedmont. They are absent in most of the upper piedmont and are scattered in the mountains. Insects and worms are the chief foods.

Spadefoots breed in shallow, temporary pools formed after very heavy, warm rains. In some localities, they fail to breed during those years when the weather is unsuitable. The call is a short, explosive, low-pitched "wank" repeated every 2 seconds. Eggs and tadpoles develop rapidly, requiring 20 to 30 days to become little toads.

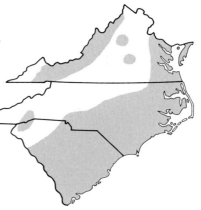

**American Toad** *Bufo americanus*

50 to 107 mm (2 to 4.25 in.) This large toad has a short broad body and a broadly circular snout. The largest specimens inhabit the mountains. The dorsum may be brown, gray, olive, or red. Although some individuals are plain, others have bright patterns, often with a light middorsal stripe. This species has large spiny warts on the dorsal surface of the hind legs, especially the shanks; one or two warts in each large dark dorsal spot; well-developed cranial crests; and conspicuous, oblong parotoid glands. Each parotoid gland is separated from the transverse crest behind the eye by a short longitudinal ridge. Dark spots occur on the anterior part of the venter. Males are smaller than females, have horny tubercles on the first and second fingers, and have dark throats.

American Toads closely resemble Southern Toads and Fowler's Toads. The Southern Toad is best identified by the large knob on its high cranial crests. Fowler's Toad has very low cranial crests, a more pointed snout, large dorsal spots enclosing three or more warts, and the parotoid gland is contiguous with the crest behind the eye.

American Toads range throughout the mountains and piedmont of North Carolina and Virginia. They also occur in the coastal plain of central North Carolina and in the mountains of South Carolina. These highly beneficial insectivores live in many habitats from

gardens to forests. In the piedmont, they are abundant only during the cooler part of the year.

In our area, they are the earliest toads to breed, February or March in the south and March or April in the north. The mating call is a long, musical, whistlelike trill, often sustained for 20 to 30 seconds. A female lays about 6,000 eggs in two long strings on the bottoms of temporary pools. Eggs hatch in less than a week and metamorphosis occurs in about 2 months. The newly transformed toads are only 7 to 12 mm long.

The parotoid glands and warts secrete a white poison that discourages many predators. The secretion can irritate a person's eyes and mouth, but toads can be handled without danger. They do not cause warts.

## Oak Toad *Bufo quercicus*

19 to 33 mm (0.75 to 1.25 in.) This dwarf among our toads is readily identified by a conspicuous light middorsal stripe and reddish orange tubercles on the undersurfaces of the hands and feet. The stripe is usually white but may be yellowish buff or reddish orange. The finely tuberculate back has four or five pairs of brown or black spots on a ground color of gray, brown, or nearly black, but these are obscure in darker toads. The dorsal tubercles are often reddish. The inflated vocal sac is ovate.

Oak Toads inhabit grassy areas in pine savannas throughout the coastal plain south of the James River in Virginia. In South Carolina they occur in maritime forests and on some barrier islands.

This abundant species breeds in the spring and summer, usually in response to heavy rains. The mating call is similar to the ''peeps'' of baby chicks. Females deposit about 700 eggs in beadlike chains of two to eight eggs in rain pools, ditches, or ponds. The transformed young are 7 to 8 mm long. Oak Toads often forage during the day.

**Southern Toad** *Bufo terrestris*

44 to 98 mm (1.75 to 4 in.) Prominent ridges and clublike knobs on the head distinguish this species. Dorsal coloration is usually brown but may be red or blackish, sometimes with a light mid-dorsal stripe. The dorsal dark spots usually contain one or two or more warts. The venter is grayish and the chest is spotted. A small bony ridge separates the parotoid gland from the postocular ridge. Females are usually lighter in color and larger than the males.

Southern Toads inhabit southeast Virginia and all the coastal plain in the Carolinas. They are abundant in a wide variety of habitats but seem to prefer areas with sandy, friable soils.

Most breeding occurs in March to May. The mating call is a long, whistlelike trill, similar to that of the American Toad but shorter in duration and an octave higher. Two long strings containing about 3,000 eggs are laid in shallow water. In a few days, the eggs hatch into tadpoles that meta-morphose in 1 to 2 months; the toadlets are 7 to 10 mm long.

**Fowler's Toad** *Bufo woodhousei*

50 to 82 mm (2 to 3.25 in.) This eastern race of Woodhouse's Toad has a brown, olive, or gray dorsum with a middorsal light stripe. Each dark dorsal spot contains three or more small warts. The cranial crests are small and contiguous with the parotoid glands. The venter is whitish, usually with a dark spot on the chest. Males have black throats and are smaller than females. Fowler's Toads sometimes hybridize with American Toads or with Southern Toads, making some specimens difficult to identify.

Fowler's Toad is abundant in most habitats of the eastern United States but is absent from the extreme southeast corner of North Carolina and most of the coastal plain in South Carolina.

Breeding occurs in March to May in the south and April to July in the north. From the edges of ponds, lakes, and streams, a male emits a loud, discordant "w-a-a-a-h" of about 1- to 4-seconds duration. A female lays about 7,000 eggs in two long strings. The eggs hatch in about a week, and the tadpoles transform 1 to 2 months later. The newly transformed toads are 8 to 11 mm long.

**Northern Cricket Frog** *Acris crepitans*

16 to 35 mm (0.5 to 1.5 in.) Cricket Frogs have moist warty skin and long legs with webs between the toes. There is a dark triangle between the eyes, and a median stripe or a Y-figure on the back, which can be bright green, russet, yellow, or shades of brown or gray. The northern species differs from the southern by having a more robust build, more webbing between the toes, a less sharply defined dark stripe on the back of the thigh and a pair of prominent, subanal, white tubercles.

This frog is a piedmont species and scarcely enters the coastal plain, except along river valleys and in the sandhills, and it is very local in major valleys in the mountains. It prefers open grassy margins of ponds, ditches, and marshy areas.

The call resembles the rapid clicking together of two small stones. Cricket Frogs breed in warm weather in shallow water. The eggs are laid singly or in small groups attached to stems or scattered on the bottom. *Acris* tadpoles have a distinctive black tail tip. Transformation occurs in late summer when the froglets are about 14 mm long.

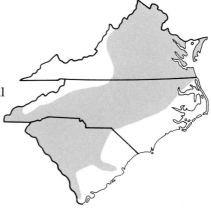

**Southern Cricket Frog** *Acris gryllus*

16 to 32 mm (0.5 to 1.5 in.) This species is very similar to the Northern Cricket Frog but is slightly smaller and more slender, the snout is more pointed, the legs longer with less webbing between the toes, and there is a sharply defined narrow black stripe on the back of the thigh. The subanal tubercles are usually indistinct.

The Southern Cricket Frog replaces the northern species in most of the coastal plain, but there is a zone along the fall line and in the sandhills where the two are sympatric. This frog is abundant on grassy margins of quasi-permanent ponds, streams, or ditches. It is a better jumper than the Northern Cricket Frog.

Though this species is active throughout the year, it breeds in late spring and summer, when its clicking calls may be heard by day or night. The eggs and tadpoles are similar to those of the Northern Cricket Frog. About 150 eggs are laid at a time, and more than one complement may be produced each year. Small insects and spiders comprise the diet.

**Pine Barrens Treefrog** *Hyla andersoni*

29 to 51 mm (1 to 2 in.) This beautiful frog is easy to identify because of the distinctive purple stripe along each side of the body. The dorsum is uniformly green, the venter is white, and the concealed surfaces of the legs are bright orange with numerous small yellow spots.

This species is known from the pine barrens of 16 counties of south central North Carolina and in the northern part of the upper coastal plain in South Carolina. It inhabits magnolias, oaks, pines, and gum trees in the low bays and upland swamps in and adjacent to the sandhills.

Most breed from April to July. Females respond to the high nasal "quonk" that is quickly repeated 10 to 20 times. Each series of calls is given at irregular intervals. The calling males are on shrubs or low trees near bogs, ditches, or slow-moving streams and are difficult to locate. In shallow water, each female lays about 500 eggs. They develop rapidly and hatch in 3 or 4 days. The newly transformed frogs are about 15 mm long.

### Bird-voiced Treefrog *Hyla avivoca*

25 to 51 mm (1 to 2 in.) This frog is similar in general proportions and pattern to the two species of Gray Treefrogs. It differs, however, by having pale greenish or yellowish white pigment on the concealed surfaces of the hind legs and groin, rather than bright orange mottled with black.

Bird-voiced Treefrogs inhabit heavily wooded swamps bordering rivers and streams. In our area they are known only from the swamps of the Savannah River and its tributaries in Aiken, Allandale, Barnwell, and Jasper counties, South Carolina.

In late spring and summer, males call from heights of 1 to 2 m on bushes and trees in or near water. The call is distinctive—a loud, rapidly repeated, birdlike whistle "whit, whit, whit." It is reminiscent of an osprey's call, or of whistling for a dog. In shallow water, a female deposits about 650 eggs in packets of 6 to 15. At high temperatures, they hatch in about 40 hours, and metamorphosis occurs in 31 to 33 days. Newly transformed frogs are about 13 mm long.

**Gray Treefrogs** *Hyla chrysoscelis*, *Hyla versicolor*

32 to 62 mm (1.25 to 2.5 in.) These two sibling or cryptic species are identical in appearance, but they do not interbreed. Genetically, they differ markedly from each other: *H. versicolor* has 48 chromosomes, twice as many as *H. chrysoscelis*. This difference is readily revealed by microscopic examination of cells of the inner eyelid (nictitating membrane). A cell of *H. chrysoscelis* has one or two nucleoli, whereas that of *H. versicolor* has three or four. During the breeding season, the two species can be identified by their calls. That of *H. chrysoscelis* is shorter, harsher, and more forceful. It contains an average of 45 trills per second, whereas that of *H. versicolor* has only 25. *H. chrysoscelis* is also reported to be slightly smaller, more tolerant of low humidity, and more arboreal. The usual color of these well-camouflaged frogs is gray, but an individual may vary from whitish to pale brown to green. Dark irregular markings occur on the upper eyelid and on the legs. The whitish mark under the eye and the bright orange on the concealed surfaces of the hind legs readily identify these frogs. The Bird-voiced Treefrog is similar but has pale green or yellowish white on the hind legs.

Gray Treefrogs range in most of the area. *H. chrysoscelis* occurs throughout the coastal plain, far into the upper piedmont, and there are several records from the mountains. The occurrence of

*H. versicolor* in parts of the mountains is suspected but not verified. These frogs forage for insects amid trees and shrubs and on the ground. Outside the breeding season (May to August), they are rarely found.

The call is a short, vibrant, flute-like trill. Scattered groups of 10 to 40 eggs are laid on the surface of shallow ditches, puddles, and ponds. Hatching occurs in 4 to 5 days and metamorphosis in 45 to 64 days. The recently transformed young are about 13 to 20 mm long.

### Green Treefrog *Hyla cinerea*

32 to 64 mm (1.25 to 2.5 in.) This large, slender treefrog has long legs and smooth skin. The venter is plain white, but the dorsum is bright or yellowish green. Most specimens have tiny golden spots on the back and a prominent light stripe on each side of the body. The stripe may be reduced or absent, especially in northern populations.

The Green Treefrog occurs throughout the coastal plain and prefers the floating and emergent vegetation along the swampy edges of ponds, lakes, marshes, and streams. During the day, these well-camouflaged frogs rest motionless, often on cattail plants; at night, they are sometimes attracted to insects near lights.

Most spawning occurs in May or June, but the mating call may be heard in April or as late as September. The call is a bell-like, nasal "queenk" repeated once a second. Each female lays about 400 eggs amid floating vegetation. The larval stage lasts about 2 months, and the newly trans- formed frogs are 12 to 17 mm long.

## Spring Peeper *Hyla crucifer*

19 to 35 mm (0.75 to 1.5 in.) This harbinger of spring has a tan, brown, or gray dorsum with a prominent dark X-shaped marking near the middle of the back and a dark barlike marking between the eyes. The underparts are buff, cream colored, or yellowish, and sometimes spotted. Males have dark throats and are usually smaller and darker than females.

Spring Peepers occur throughout the area. They inhabit woodlands and live under forest litter or amid brushy undergrowth.

Breeding occurs in woodland ponds, swamps, and ditches from October to March in the southern coastal regions but from February to May in the northern and mountainous areas. The call—a clear, high-pitched (birdlike) "peep" ending with an upward slur—is repeated about once a second. The eggs (about 900 per complement) are attached singly to submerged objects. The eggs hatch in a few days and metamorphosis occurs 3 to 4 months later. Their diet consists primarily of small arthropods, and in turn they may fall prey to large spiders.

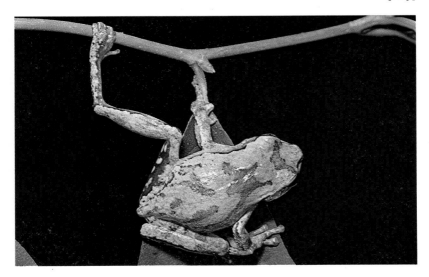

**Pine Woods Treefrog** *Hyla femoralis*

25 to 38 mm (1 to 1.5 in.) This slender frog is usually brown with dark markings on its back, but individuals vary from pale gray to dark brown. Small yellow or orange spots against a dark background on the rear of the thigh provide a diagnostic feature. The Bird-voiced and the two Gray Treefrogs are similar, but these species have a prominent white spot just below the eye.

This well-named species lives in pine flatwoods and savannas, usually near bogs or ponds. It is occasionally found in hardwood forests and swamps. Pine Woods Treefrogs occur throughout most of the coastal plain.

The Pine Woods Treefrog breeds in the late spring and summer. The mating call, emitted by males on trees in the water, is a low-pitched, guttural trill, which sounds somewhat like "getta, getta." It is often heard in pine savannas on dark overcast days. Females deposit films of 100 to 125 eggs on the water's surface or just below it on stems or other objects. The tadpole stage lasts 50 to 75 days; transformed young are about 13 mm long.

## Barking Treefrog *Hyla gratiosa*

51 to 69 mm (2 to 2.75 in.) This large, very stout frog usually has prominent circular dorsal spots on a background of pale greenish gray to bright green or dark brown. In the extremely light or very dark phases, the dorsal spots may be obscure. The belly is white or yellowish white.

Barking Treefrogs are common locally in sandy areas near shallow ponds in pine savannas and in low wet woods and swamps. They occur throughout most of the coastal plain and in portions of the adjacent piedmont of the Carolinas.

This species is active in the late spring and summer. Breeding occurs in shallow ponds after heavy rains. As the males move into the ponds from bushes or trees, they utter series of loud, distinctive, doglike barks, but when the water is entered, the call changes to a hollow-sounding "doonk" repeated at short intervals. Females deposit eggs singly on the bottom of the pond; the total egg complement is about 2,000. The tadpole stage lasts 40 to 70 days; transformed young are 14 to 20 mm long.

**Squirrel Treefrog** *Hyla squirella*

22 to 41 mm (1 to 1.5 in.) This frog can rapidly change its color and markings. The dorsum is usually dull brown with many or few round dark spots or may be light or bright green and unspotted. There is at least a partial bar between the eyes and a whitish line on the upper lip, shoulder, and side of body. The belly is whitish with a suffusion of yellow on axilla, groin, thigh, and shank. This species differs from other *Hyla* in that it lacks a light spot under the eye, a dark X marking on the back, and yellow or orange spots on the thigh.

This common frog prefers open woods but often occurs around buildings in cities and towns. It ranges from southeastern Virginia throughout the coastal plain and sporadically in the adjacent piedmont.

Breeding is associated with summer storms. The call is a flat, nasal, ducklike "waaaak," 0.25 second long and repeated every 0.5 second. A female lays about 1,000 eggs on the bottom of open ponds or pools. Tadpoles transform after 45 days, and the new frogs average 12 mm from snout to vent. Small insects are the chief food.

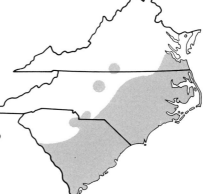

### Little Grass Frog *Limnaoedus ocularis*

13 to 19 mm (0.5 to 0.75 in.) This diminutive frog, the smallest in North America, varies from gray to brown or brick red. A dark stripe extends from the nostril through the eye onto the sides, and a dark middorsal stripe is sometimes present. The belly is yellowish white. In late spring, Little Grass Frogs can be confused with the young of Brimley's and Southern Chorus Frogs, but inflated vocal sacs in males or eggs showing through the belly in females will distinguish this species.

Little Grass Frogs prefer grassy areas near bogs or ponds in pine savannas, and pools or streams in hardwood forests and swamps. They occur in most of the coastal plain.

This abundant species breeds in association with spring and summer rains, but its insectlike mating calls may be heard in warm weather throughout much of the year. Females deposit about 100 eggs singly on the bottom of shallow ponds or in vegetation. Transformation occurs after a tadpole stage of 45 to 70 days; recently transformed young are 7 to 9 mm long.

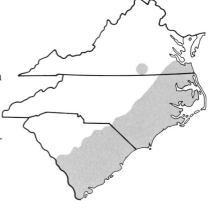

**Mountain Chorus Frog** *Pseudacris brachyphona*

25 to 38 mm (1 to 1.5 in.) The brown or gray dorsum has a dark mark between the eyes and a pair of irregular lateral markings that are sometimes connected near the midback to form a thickened H-like pattern. The venter is whitish; only males have dark throats. This species differs from other chorus frogs by having a stockier body, a wide head, large digital pads, and no middorsal stripe or spots. It resembles the Spring Peeper but has smaller toe pads and a white line on the upper lip.

Mountain Chorus Frogs inhabit wooded areas in southwestern North Carolina and western Virginia.

Breeding occurs from February to April. The mating call is a harsh, raspy "wreenk" or "reek" and may be heard day or night. The 400 eggs in the average complement are laid in groups of 10 to 50 and are attached to vegetation in shallow quiet ponds, ditches, and small pools along the edges of streams. The eggs hatch in 4 or 5 days, and the hatchlings are 5 mm in total length. Tadpoles reach a total length of 30 mm and transform in 50 to 56 days. The froglets average 8 mm long.

**Brimley's Chorus Frog** *Pseudacris brimleyi*

25 to 32 mm (1 to 1.25 in.) This small tan frog has three brown stripes on its back and a distinct dark brown or black stripe on each side extending from the nostril through the eye to the groin. On some individuals the dorsal stripes may be obscure. The under-surface is yellow, and the chest is usually spotted with brown. This species is readily distinguished from the coastal plain form of the Upland Chorus Frog by the horizontal brown stripe on the rear of its shank.

Brimley's Chorus Frogs inhabit low areas in hardwood forests and swamps near rivers and streams. They occur in the coastal plain, but do not reach north-eastern Virginia.

This abundant species breeds in the winter and early spring. The mating call is a short, gutteral trill, somewhat similar to that of the Squirrel Treefrog. Females deposit small loose clusters of eggs on stems or other objects in ditches or shallow ponds. The tadpole stage probably lasts 40 to 60 days; trans-formed young are 9 to 11 mm long.

**Southern Chorus Frog** *Pseudacris nigrita*

19 to 32 mm (0.75 to 1.25 in.) This small gray frog has a prominent black stripe on each side from the snout to the groin and three rows of irregular black spots on the back. The belly is usually white. A distinct silvery or yellowish white stripe usually extends along the upper lip. Upland Chorus Frogs are similar, but have yellowish bellies spotted with brown, a tan or brown back, and often a dark triangular spot between the eyes, which may be absent in coastal plain frogs.

When active, this pine savanna species calls from ditches, bogs, and shallow ponds. It occurs throughout most of the coastal plain in the Carolinas.

Southern Chorus Frogs breed from late fall to early spring. The mating call is an ascending trill, similar to the sound produced by scraping the teeth of a comb. Females deposit small irregular egg clusters on stems, leaves, or other objects in shallow water. The tadpole stage lasts about 50 days; recently transformed young are about 9 to 15 mm long.

## Ornate Chorus Frog *Pseudacris ornata*

25 to 38 mm (1 to 1.5 in.) This colorful frog may be tan or green but is usually brick red. The concealed surfaces of the thigh and groin are usually bright yellow. A dark, triangular spot is often present between the eyes, and there are prominent black spots along the sides, on the lower back, and in the groin. A bold black stripe extends from the nostril through the eye to the shoulder on each side.

Ornate Chorus Frogs inhabit pine savannas and swamps; breeding males call from flooded fields, ditches, and shallow ponds. They occur throughout most of the coastal plain in the Carolinas.

This abundant species breeds in the fall and winter. The mating call is a series of loud, metallic, bird-like peeps, resembling the trill of the Spring Peeper but lacking its ascending quality. Females deposit small irregular clusters of 10 to 100 eggs on stems or other objects in shallow water. The recently transformed young are 14 to 16 mm long.

## Upland Chorus Frog *Pseudacris triseriata*

19 to 35 mm (0.75 to 1.5 in.) The dorsum is brown or gray with a variable pattern. A distinct stripe extends from snout through eye to groin, and the three dorsal stripes may be reduced to rows of spots. A dark marking lies between the eyes and a light one lines the upper lip. The venter is granular and cream colored, often with dark stippling on the chest. The toes have small pads and little or no webbing.

This species occurs at low elevations in the mountains, widely throughout the piedmont and upper coastal plain, but only sporadically in the lower coastal plain of the Carolinas.

They breed in semipermanent pools from December to March in the south and February to May in the north. The mating call is a regularly repeated "crrreek" imitated by thumbnailing the teeth of a comb. A female lays about 1,000 eggs. These are laid in clusters of about 60 each and are attached to vegetation. The tadpole state lasts 2 to 3 months; average size at metamorphosis is 9.5 mm. These forest-floor dwellers eat small arthropods.

**Crawfish Frog** *Rana areolata*

72 to 94 mm (2.75 to 3.5 in.) This large, toadlike frog has a wide
mouth and cobblestone rows of prominent warts on its back. The
belly is heavily mottled with dark spots or flecks, and the concealed surfaces of the thigh and groin are suffused with yellow.
The back is dark gray with relatively prominent dorsolateral folds.

Crawfish Frogs inhabit dry, turkey oak–pine associations and
other sandy areas in pine savannas. They are uncommon, highly
terrestrial, and enter water only to breed. When not active on the
surface, these frogs occupy the burrows of crayfish and other
animals. The range of this species extends north in the coastal
plain to Beaufort County, North
Carolina.

Crawfish Frogs are explosive
breeders, entering pine savanna
ponds in late winter to early fall
after very heavy rains. The mating
call, a deep, humanlike snore, is
sometimes given under water. The
egg mass is a large globular cluster
attached to stems. The tadpole
stage lasts 85 to 100 days; transformed young are 27 to 38 mm
long.

## Bullfrog *Rana catesbeiana*

85 to 200 mm (3.5 to 8 in.) This is our largest frog. The dorsum is olive or brown with large obscure blotches on the adults and many small black dots on the young. The venter is buffy white with dark reticulations or mottling. Bullfrogs lack a dorsolateral fold but have a thin fold alongside the tympanum. Males are smaller than females and have a yellow throat and larger tympanum, thumb, and forearm. River Frogs have rougher skin and light spots on the upper lip. Pig Frogs have a more pointed snout and more webbing between the toes.

Bullfrogs are common in the Carolinas and Virginia. They are wary and solitary, preferring large ponds, lakes, and streams.

The vibrant, deep bass "jug-o'-rum" can be heard great distances during late spring and early summer. About 12,000 eggs are laid by each female. They hatch in 5 days, and metamorphosis usually occurs a year later. Some tadpoles reach a very large size (total length of 125 to 150 mm). Insects, crayfish, and sometimes small vertebrates are eaten.

**Green Frog** *Rana clamitans*

54 to 86 mm (2 to 3.5 in.) The Green Frog's dorsolateral folds extend only to the middle of the back. The dorsum is green or brown, usually with obscure dark spots. Most specimens from the coastal plain of South Carolina and southeastern North Carolina have a plain brown back and lack green on the upper lip. The venter is white but dark markings usually occur on the chin, breast, and hind legs, especially on young frogs. The male has a large tympanum, yellow throat, and stout foreleg and thumb.

Green Frogs live along streams, ponds, and lakes throughout the Carolinas and Virginia. A high-pitched "squeenk" is often given as a startled frog jumps to safety.

Most breed in May and June. The call is a low, explosive, twangy "c'tung." About 3,000 eggs are laid in a raftlike surface film. Most tadpoles transform in a few months, but some overwinter. Sexual maturity occurs near the end of the first full summer after metamorphosis. Mainly arthropods, snails, and worms are eaten.

## Pig Frog *Rana grylio*

80 to 162 mm (3 to 6.25 in.) Pig Frogs resemble Bullfrogs but have a narrower, more pointed snout, conspicuous light and dark horizontal bands on the rear of the thigh, and more fully webbed hind feet. Young Pig Frogs are similar to adult Carpenter Frogs. To distinguish them, note that the Pig Frog's longest toe is webbed nearly to its tip, but in Bullfrogs and Carpenter Frogs the webbing extends only to the midpoint of the last joint.

This species prefers large, open, relatively shallow ponds or lakes with lily pads and much emergent vegetation. It is abundant in abandoned rice fields and rice field reservoirs. Pig Frogs occur in the South Carolina coastal plain north to Georgetown County.

The common name of this frog stems from its distinctive mating call, an explosive, piglike grunt; breeding choruses occur from early April to early August. Each female deposits about 10,000 eggs in a thin layer on the surface of the water. The tadpole stage lasts about 1 year; transformed young are 32 to 49 mm long.

**River Frog** *Rana heckscheri*

80 to 135 mm (3 to 5.25 in.) This large dark brown frog has conspicuous white spots on the margins of its jaws and a belly usually heavily mottled with black. It may be confused with dark Bullfrogs, but in these the pale areas of the belly are larger and the jaws lack white spots. Green Frogs are sometimes similar but have dorsolateral folds.

River Frogs inhabit bottomland forests and swamps of rivers and streams. They occur throughout the coastal plain north to the Lumber and Cape Fear rivers in North Carolina.

This species breeds in the late spring and early summer. The mating call is a deep, trainlike snore, but territorial males may also voice a loud, explosive grunt. Females deposit eggs, probably as a surface film, in ponds near rivers or streams. The very large tadpole, which reaches a length of 97 mm, has a tail fin conspicuously edged with black. The tadpole stage probably lasts 2 years; recently transformed young are 30 to 52 mm long.

**Pickerel Frog** *Rana palustris*

44 to 87 mm (1.75 to 3.5 in.) This moderately large frog has dorso-lateral folds and two rows of squarish spots on the back. In coastal plain individuals, the spots often merge to form short oblong bars or broad elongate stripes. The belly is white in mountain and piedmont frogs, and mottled with brown in coastal plain ones. The concealed surfaces of the thigh and groin are bright yellow to orange. Southern Leopard Frogs have oval spots on the back and no yellow or orange on the thigh and groin.

This species lives in a variety of aquatic habitats in wooded areas, including bogs and grassy places near shaded streams. They occur throughout the Carolinas and Virginia, but populations are widely disjunct.

Most Pickerel Frogs breed during the late winter and early spring, usually with the advent of heavy rains. The mating call is a low-pitched snore. Females deposit globular clusters of about 2,500 eggs on stems in ponds or pools. The tadpole stage lasts 70 to 80 days; transformed young are 19 to 27 mm long.

**Southern Leopard Frog** *Rana sphenocephala*

50 to 90 mm (2 to 3.5 in.) The dorsum of these long-legged, active frogs is green or brown or both, with large rounded dark spots; in contrast, the venter is white. Distinct dorsolateral folds extend the full length of the body. Males are smaller than females and have paired vocal sacs and enlarged forearms and thumbs. Unlike the Northern Leopard Frog (of the Northeast and Midwest), this species is smaller, has a longer, pointed head, a light spot in the center of the tympanum, no snout spot, and fewer dark spots on the sides of the body. Males lack vestigial oviducts and possess external vocal sacs. The Pickerel Frog is similar to the Southern Leopard Frog but has more angular dorsal spots and bright yellow or orange color on the concealed and ventral surfaces of the hindlegs.

Southern Leopard Frogs occur mainly in the coastal plain but penetrate into the mountains of South Carolina. They inhabit ponds, ditches, and swamps, as well as the margins of lakes and streams. They forage on land, primarily for insects, and often travel far from water.

This species usually breeds in the winter or early spring but occasionally in the fall. The call is a series of three to five guttural croaks followed by two or three "clucks." It suggests the sounds made by rubbing an inflated balloon. The calling males are wary and difficult to approach. Each female attaches a firm cluster (about 90 mm wide and 40 mm thick) of several hundred eggs to vegetation just below the water's surface. Breeding Leopard Frogs often congregate and lay numerous clusters of eggs in a small area. In a week or two, eggs hatch into tadpoles about 20 to 25 mm long. About 3 months later, the average tadpole is 65 to 70 mm long, its tail bears prominent dark spots, and metamorphosis is imminent. The newly formed frogs are about 20 mm long.

## Wood Frog *Rana sylvatica*

35 to 83 mm (1.5 to 3.25 in.) This medium-sized frog is easily identified by its mask, a dark patch extending back from the eye. The
dorsum varies from light to reddish to dark brown. The females are
more brightly colored and much larger than the males. The venter
is white with a dark spot on each side of the chest. Dorsolateral
folds are prominent.

Wood Frogs live in or near moist woods often far from open
water. In the Carolinas, they inhabit only the mountains and upper
piedmont; in Virginia they are scattered throughout the piedmont
and the northern part of the upper coastal plain.

Breeding is usually limited to a few days in February when large
numbers aggregate. The mating
call, a rasping "craw-aw-auk," has
little carrying power. The globular
egg masses are often closely aggre-
gated and attached to plants below
the surface of a shallow pond or
pool. After 40 to 50 days, the
tadpoles transform. These frogs
feed chiefly on beetles and flies.
They hibernate under leaves or
logs in wooded ravines.

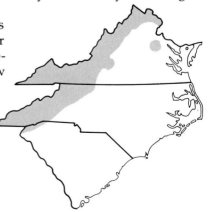

**Carpenter Frog** *Rana virgatipes*

41 to 67 mm (1.5 to 2.5 in.) This small frog has four yellowish brown stripes, two on the back and one on each side. The rear of the thigh has alternating light and dark stripes and the belly is usually mottled with black. Young Pig Frogs are similar but their longest toe is webbed nearly to its tip; in Carpenter Frogs, two joints of the longest toe are free of webbing.

Carpenter Frogs are often difficult to capture or observe, for they blend in well against sphagnum mats and other vegetation in the coffee-colored waters of the pine savanna bogs or ponds in which they live. This species occurs throughout most of the coastal plain.

This frog breeds in the spring and summer. The mating call, an explosive two-noted "clack-it," is repeated three to six times in rapid succession and resembles the sound of a distant carpenter nailing shingles. The egg mass is a flattened or globular cluster containing 200 to 600 eggs. The tadpole stage lasts about 1 year; transformed young are 23 to 31 mm long.

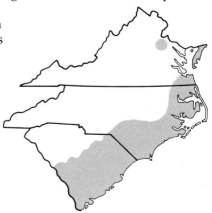

**Eastern Narrowmouth Toad** *Gastrophryne carolinensis*

22 to 38 mm (1 to 1.5 in.) These small stocky toads have smooth skin, a pointed snout, and a unique fold of skin across the back of the head. The dorsum may be gray, brown, or reddish and has a broad dark central marking. The venter is heavily speckled or mottled, and males have dark throats. The absence of parotoid glands, warts, and webs between the toes distinguishes these toads from other species.

Narrowmouth Toads occur throughout the coastal plain and lower piedmont but are absent from most of the mountains and upper piedmont. The adults are terrestrial, secretive ant eaters. They spend much time in burrows and are sometimes found under logs, rocks, and boards.

During warm rains in May to July, large numbers aggregate in shallow puddles, ponds, streams, and swamps. The mating call is a prolonged, lamblike nasal "baaaa." Packets of eggs are laid on the surface of the water; each comple-ment contains about 850 eggs. In 20 to 70 days, metamorphosis oc-curs; the new frogs measure 8.5 to 12 mm long.

# Class Reptilia

Reptiles evolved from primitive amphibians about 300 million years ago. The oldest fossils are from the Pennsylvanian period of the Paleozoic era. Reptiles were the first vertebrates to become completely free of the aquatic environment. By the Mesozoic era they became the dominant vertebrates and radiated not only in terrestrial environments but also in marine, fresh water, and aerial habitats as well. In the Mesozoic, these highly successful animals gave rise to the birds and mammals, but by the close of that era, 12 of the 16 orders had become extinct. Only 4 orders are living today: Chelonia (turtles), Crocodilia (crocodiles, alligators, and their kin), Rhynchocephalia (1 relict species native to the New Zealand area), and Squamata (lizards and snakes).

Reptiles have a dry, glandless skin covered with horny scales. Snakes and a few lizards are legless, but basically reptiles have two pairs of limbs each with five clawed digits. Fertilization in all reptiles is internal. Some snakes and lizards give birth to young, but most reptiles lay large eggs provided with an enormous yolk and a protective shell. Unlike the eggs of fish and amphibians, the reptile egg is specialized for development on land. In addition to the *yolk sac*, a primitive membrane that permits a vertebrate embryo to use nutrients stored in the egg, reptiles and their descendents have three additional membranes: the *amnion* surrounds the embryo and secretes a fluid that suspends and protects the embryo; the *allantois*, a large saclike extension of the digestive tube, is vascular and stores metabolic wastes and is also a respiratory surface; and the *serosa* encloses the developing young and the other membranes. The shell is leathery or lime impregnated. Its porosity allows exchange of respiratory gases and the uptake of water. It protects the embryo from physical pressures and desiccation. Unlike fish and many amphibians, reptiles lack gills, have no free-living larval stage, and breathe solely by means of lungs. Studies of reptilian genetics have been greatly discouraged because in many species the females store sperm for long periods; some have produced viable young 5 years after copulation.

About 6,000 species of reptiles are living today. They are most numerous in the tropics and subtropics but a few live near the Arctic Circle and at high altitudes (up to 4,900 m) in the Himalayas and Andes mountains. Even though they are not warm-blooded, many reptiles maintain a surprisingly high body temperature within narrow limits. This is accomplished mainly by behavioral means such as basking, orientation, postural changes, and habitat selection; however, some also use limited physiological means: panting, vasomotor responses, and metabolic heat production.

## Order Crocodilia = Loricata

CROCODILES AND ALLIGATORS

About 200 million years ago the Crocodilia evolved from the Thecodontia (Triassic reptiles with teeth firmly set in sockets). They flourished in the Jurassic and Cretaceous, but now include only 21 living species. Modern crocodilians are relatively similar in general body shape and in habits. They are medium to very large, the adults ranging in total length from 1 to almost 7 m. All have long powerful jaws equipped with large teeth set in deep sockets, a long muscular tail, and two pairs of limbs. Each front foot has the usual five toes, but each hind foot has only four toes. Very large horny scales cover the body, and many, especially those on the back, contain plates of dermal bone. Crocodilians are well equipped for semiaquatic living; the nostrils and ear openings are valvelike and close when submerged, and the heart rate may drop from about 28 to 5 beats per minute. A diaphragmlike septum separates the lungs from the abdominal viscera, and a bony palate separates the nasal passage from the mouth. The heart in most modern species has a complete septum between the ventricles, as occurs in birds and mammals. Indeed, modern crocodilians are more closely related to birds than to other living reptiles.

These predators eat a wide variety of organisms, ranging from small invertebrates to large mammals. Some crocodilians are territorial, and many species produce a deep, rumbling bellow. Males have a single median copulatory organ. Most species lay 14 to 100 eggs per clutch in mound-shaped nests constructed of soil and vegetation; however, a few dig holes for their eggs. Unlike most other reptiles, crocodilians often actively defend the eggs and the very young from predators. In some species, the female assists the hatchlings by opening the nest and gently carrying them in her mouth to water.

Because their skins are commercially valuable and because a few of the larger species may be dangerous to man, crocodilians have been eagerly hunted. This persecution has been exacerbated by man's continuing destruction of their habitat. Some species are perilously close to extinction, and for some of them recent protective measures may be too late. In contrast, the American Alligator has shown great resiliency under protection during the last decade. They have become so abundant that they are a nuisance in some parts of more southern states.

Crocodilians are chiefly tropical and only the American and Chinese alligators occur in the north temperate zone. The former is the only crocodilian native to our area. The Spectacled Caiman has been extensively imported from Central and South America for the pet trade. After the novelty wears off, many of these animals are released. Although some may survive for several years, there is no evidence that any reproduce in our area.

**American Alligator** *Alligator mississippiensis*

1.8 to 5.8 m (6 to 19 ft.) This large reptile has a broad snout, a short
neck, a heavy body, and a laterally compressed tail. Adults are
blackish or dark gray, but faint yellowish crossbands are sometimes
evident. The young are black with conspicuous yellow crossbands.
The Spectacled Caiman is similar, but has a small, curved bony
ridge in front of the eyes.

The American Alligator inhabits fresh water swamps, marshes,
abandoned rice fields, ponds, lakes, and backwaters of large rivers.
Although its range once extended north in the coastal plain to

Dismal Swamp, the American Alligator is now absent in the area north of Albemarle Sound and in much of the upper coastal plain.

In June, the female builds a large mound of leaves, mud, and debris about 60 cm high, 120 to 200 cm wide, and usually located in a shaded area a few meters from the water. She deposits about 30 eggs in a cavity atop the mound, remains nearby, and challenges all intruders, frequently including man. Hatchlings about 21 cm long emerge in late summer or early fall.

# Order Chelonia = Testudinata

TURTLES

Turtles are the most ancient of all living reptiles. They are evolutionarily conservative and have changed little since their origin early in the Triassic period. These unique vertebrates possess a shell, a protective structure composed of an upper part, called the carapace, and a lower part, the plastron. The shells of most species are bony and covered with horny scutes. Unlike those of other vertebrates, the limb girdles are enclosed in the greatly expanded rib cage. The feet are elephantine in highly terrestrial forms, webbed in the aquatic ones, or modified as flippers in those that live in the open seas. The jaws lack teeth and are covered by a horny beak. Adults of modern species range in carapace length from about 70 mm to 2 m.

Most turtles are omnivorous, but some are carnivorous and a few are herbivorous. In some species, the juveniles are carnivorous and become herbivorous as adults. Most species court and mate in the fall as well as in the spring. All species are oviparous. The eggs are usually laid in a hole dug in the soil. Most species oviposit in late spring, but some also lay one or more times in the summer. The eggs in a clutch vary from 1 to about 300, depending on the species. In Virginia and the Carolinas, hatching usually takes place in late summer or fall, and the young of several species may overwinter in the nest.

Man interacts with turtles in many ways. He eats their flesh and eggs and prepares numerous products from their skins, shells, and bones. Live turtles, especially hatchlings, once constituted a lucrative part of the pet trade. Like many organisms, turtles are adversely affected by man's general destruction of the habitat: drainage, pollution, land clearing, and strip mining. Without doubt, the automobile is one of the greatest threats to turtles, and each year many thousands are killed on the roads. Several species are threatened with extinction, and only a few are protected by law.

Most of the 220 modern species occur in the warmer parts of the world but 24 species are native to the Carolinas and Virginia. All but 2 of our species (Gopher Tortoise and Box Turtle) are chiefly or highly aquatic. The Emydidae includes 12 species and is the largest family. The genus *Chrysemys* has 5 species, *Clemmys* has 3, *Sternotherus* and *Trionyx* have 2 each, and each of the other 12 genera has 1 species.

**Snapping Turtle** *Chelydra serpentina*

200 to 470 mm (8 to 18.5 in.) These big brownish turtles are mean and aggressive. They attain weights up to 26 kg (57 lbs.) but can get much larger in captivity. Their most outstanding features include: large head; long tapering tail armed above with large scales; small, cross-shaped plastron; and carapace with three longitudinal keels prominent in the young. In males, the cloaca lies posterior to the edge of the shell, in females anterior.

Snapping Turtles are common in most fresh water habitats throughout the area. They occasionally enter brackish water. Under water, they usually do not bite, but on land even hatchlings snap savagely at imposing objects. Aquatic invertebrates, numerous small vertebrates, and aquatic plants are the dietary staples.

In early spring, adults wander from one body of water to another. In late spring, about 25 eggs per clutch are laid in a shallow nest, sometimes a considerable distance from water. The eggs are spherical and hatch in 3 months; the young have a carapace length of 25 to 30 mm. The flesh of this species is a popular ingredient of soups and stews.

**Eastern Mud Turtle** *Kinosternon subrubrum*

75 to 124 mm (3 to 5 in.) This small turtle is appropriately named, reflecting both its color and habitat. It differs from the Eastern Musk Turtle by lacking stripes on the head, and the pectoral scutes meet only narrowly on the midline of the plastron, which is hinged both before and after the abdominal scutes.

It is an abundant turtle in the coastal plain and prefers the quiet waters of creeks, ditches, ponds, and lakes. It even tolerates brackish water and occurs both on the Delmarva Peninsula and on the outer banks. It becomes increasingly scarce across the piedmont and avoids the mountains.

Mud Turtles usually hide by day and forage under water at night. Insects, mollusks, carrion, and vegetation are the major dietary items. In late spring, the female digs a nest in soft soil near the water, and deposits three to five elliptical eggs. Hatching occurs about 100 days later, but the young may remain nestbound until the next spring.

## Stripeneck Musk Turtle *Sternotherus minor*

75 to 114 mm (3 to 4.5 in.) This small turtle has dark stripes on the head and neck, a relatively high brown or gray carapace with dark markings, and a yellowish, usually unspotted plastron. The carapace of juveniles usually bears a distinct middorsal keel and traces of an additional keel on each side. Adults typically lack carapacial keels. There are two barbels on the chin but none on the throat. The Eastern Musk Turtle is similar, but has prominent white stripes on the head and barbels on the chin and throat.

Stripeneck Musk Turtles are highly aquatic. They inhabit swamps, rivers, streams, and springs, preferring muddy bottoms near submerged logs or other objects. This species is known in the area only from extreme southwestern Virginia.

This active turtle is diurnal and forages mainly during the morning hours. It is omnivorous, but prefers aquatic insects and snails. The natural history of this species is poorly known.

## Eastern Musk Turtle *Sternotherus odoratus*

80 to 136 mm (3 to 5.5 in.) This drab little turtle is noted for its musky odor, a warning to predators. Its head bears two pairs of barbels on the chin and throat, and a light line above the eye and another below the eye. These lines may be obscure or lost in old males. The plastron is small and the suture between the humeral scutes (anterior pair) is about as long as that between the pectorals (second pair). In the Mud Turtle, the pectoral suture is much shorter and the pectorals are triangular. Only the anterior lobe of the plastron is hinged.

This musk turtle is abundant in ponds and streams in the coastal plain and lower piedmont but is scarce in the upper piedmont and in mountain valleys. It prefers soft bottoms, where it will hibernate buried in the mud.

It is omnivorous, with insects and snails the most common foods. The two to five eggs are white, brittle, elliptical, and about 27 mm long. They are laid in soft dirt or humus very close to the water. The hatchlings are 21 mm long and triangular in cross section.

### River Cooter *Chrysemys concinna*

140 to 320 mm (5.5 to 12.5 in.) The River Cooter is very similar to the Florida Cooter, but its shell is flatter and the light dorsal markings form a pattern that is more reticulate or concentric, usually with a light C-shaped mark on the first or second pleural scute. There generally are irregular dark figures on the plastron along the seams between the scutes. The long fore claws of the mature male, present in all species of *Chrysemys*, are used to stroke the head of the female during courtship.

This species is scarce over the coastal plain of our states. Since it favors rivers with moderate current, it penetrates higher into the piedmont than does the Florida Cooter.

The nesting and feeding habits of the River Cooter approximate those of the Florida Cooter. The ecological and genetic interactions between these two species in our area are complex and deserve careful study. Hybridization occurs frequently, and some specimens defy classification at the species level.

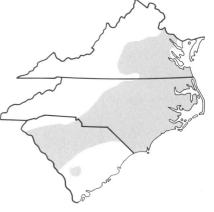

## Florida Cooter *Chrysemys floridana*

220 to 397 mm (9 to 15.5 in.) Florida Cooters are large turtles with rugose dark shells bearing transverse light marks that branch irregularly. The plastron is immaculate yellow except on the bridge. The head and neck are striped with yellow and the hind limbs have both vertical and horizontal yellow markings posteriorly. Adult males have long needlelike foreclaws (see account of the River Cooter).

This is a lowland turtle preferring the quiet waters of canals, lakes, and slow rivers and an abundance of vegetation. On the piedmont, it is found in impoundments and farm ponds.　·

A female lays about 20 elliptical eggs per clutch and usually produces two clutches a year. The eggs average about 25 by 34 mm. Nests are dug in light soil in open areas near water. Hatching takes place in about 90 days. Emergence from late nests may be delayed until the next spring. The young grow 2 to 4 cm a year until mature—males in 3 years, females in 6 years. Adults are largely herbivorous, the young omnivorous.

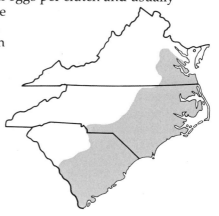

**Painted Turtle** *Chrysemys picta*

114 to 180 mm (4.5 to 7 in.) Painted Turtles in our area have pale seams between the dorsal scutes on a dark brown, greenish, or black carapace, two yellow spots in line behind the eye, and conspicuous red markings around the edge of the shell. The dark skin is striped with red and yellow. Males are smaller than females and have elongated nails on the fore limbs which are used to stroke the face of the female during courtship.

Painted Turtles occur throughout most of our area but are widely scattered in the mountains and absent from the coastal plain of South Carolina and southeastern North Carolina. They are favorite pets and have been introduced in many localities. They prefer quiet waters with muddy bottoms and plentiful vegetation and are omnivorous feeders. Individuals commonly bask on logs or stumps or float at the surface of the water. Estimates of over 200 turtles per acre of water have been reported.

Nesting occurs in early summer when 2 to 10 eggs are laid. They require about 75 days to hatch.

### Redbelly Turtle *Chrysemys rubriventris*

250 to 400 mm (10 to 16 in.) The Redbelly Turtle has a median notch on the upper jaw flanked by a cusp on either side, and both jaws are strongly serrate on the cutting edges. The plastron is reddish and usually bears dark smudges or a symmetrical marking. The marginal and pleural scutes have dull red vertical bars through their centers; the bars may be obscure in old specimens. The top of the head has an arrow formed by a median light stripe and lines from the eyes on the tip of the snout. The closely related Florida and River Cooters lack the reddish tones and the arrow on the head, and their upper jaw edges are nearly smooth.

This large basking turtle occurs from well up along the Potomac River in eastern Virginia to Pamlico Sound in North Carolina. Hybridization with the Florida Cooter has been reported from the Albemarle Peninsula in North Carolina. Egg complements of 10 to 35 are laid in suitable soil near the water in early to midsummer. Young emerge in late summer or the next spring.

### Yellowbelly Slider *Chrysemys scripta*

125 to 290 mm (5 to 11.5 in.) Young Yellowbelly Sliders have dark shells with prominent light transverse bars on each side. These become obscure in many specimens, and old males are nearly black. A large yellow vertical spot behind the eye linking a pair of yellow stripes on each side of the neck is diagnostic of this turtle. The plastron is yellow and usually has a pair of dark spots on the gular (anterior) scutes, and often additional ones on more posterior scutes. The posterior thighs are barred vertically with yellow and black. Adult males are smaller than adult females and have elongated nails on the fore limbs.

This turtle is abundant in the coastal plain and piedmont. It has also been reported from Tazewell County, Virginia.

It is fond of basking, especially in early spring. Nesting occurs in May and June when females leave the water to find suitable sites for nests. About 10 eggs are laid which hatch in about 2 months. This species is omnivorous, but juveniles are more carnivorous than adults.

**Spotted Turtle** *Clemmys guttata*

89 to 127 mm (3.5 to 5 in.) These small blackish turtles are easily recognized by the bright orange or yellow spots on the head and carapace. The male has brown eyes and a tan or pale brown chin, the female yellow eyes and a yellow chin. Carapacial spots of juveniles are few or sometimes absent.

This colorful species occurs throughout the coastal plain and in some sections of the lower piedmont. Favorite habitats are damp meadows and pastures, swamps, small streams, and other shallow bodies of water. The Spotted Turtle is especially vulnerable to habitat disruption resulting from drainage and development.

These turtles are most active in the spring, and some individuals may be abroad during warm periods in the winter. They usually are difficult to find in the summer. Plants and small animals, especially invertebrates, are the main foods. A female deposits from three to six eggs in late spring or summer, and hatching takes place in late summer or fall. The carapace of hatchlings is about 30 mm long.

**Wood Turtle** *Clemmys insculpta*

140 to 230 mm (5.5 to 9 in.) This rare turtle is distinguished by its rough carapace. Each dorsal scute is a raised pyramid of concentric ridges and increases in height with age. The tail is long, and the forelegs and neck of adults are usually marked below with orange. The yellow plastron has a prominent dark blotch on the posterior corner of each scute.

The Wood Turtle is a northern species ranging from Canada south only to the northern tier of counties in Virginia. It has a restricted home range and is more or less terrestrial and diurnal. It forages through deciduous woods, bogs, and fields in normal weather, but in dry periods it moves to water. It eats algae, grasses, leaves, berries, insects, mollusks, earthworms, and tad-poles.

The female digs a nest with her hind legs as deep as their length permits, wherein she deposits 4 to 12 eggs, each about 40 mm long. Young of 30 to 35 mm carapace length may emerge in the fall after about 2.5 months, but sometimes they overwinter in the nest.

**Bog Turtle** *Clemmys muhlenbergi*

76 to 102 mm (3 to 4 in.) This is our smallest turtle. It has a dark
brown carapace and a blackish plastron. The bright orange or
yellow blotch on each side of the head and neck makes identification easy. Sexual dimorphism is not striking; the female has a
shorter tail than the male and a flatter plastron with a wide notch
at its posterior margin.

The Bog Turtle occurs in the mountains and upper piedmont of
North Carolina and southern Virginia. These secretive turtles are
generally rare and widely scattered. They inhabit damp grassy
fields, bogs, and marshes. When
disturbed, they quickly burrow
into mud or debris.

Bog Turtles eat mostly insects,
but also eat worms, snails, amphibians, and seeds. In June or
July, three to five eggs are laid in
a shallow nest in moss or loose
soil. They hatch about 55 days
later, and the young average about
25 mm in carapace length.

**Chicken Turtle** *Deirochelys reticularia*

100 to 250 mm (4 to 10 in.) A very long neck and narrow shell identify this uncommon turtle. The forelimb bears a unique broad yellow band, and the posterior surface of the thighs is barred vertically with yellow on black, a character shared only with the Yellow-belly Slider. The yellow plastron is often unmarked, but there are usually one or two elongate black blotches on the bridge. The dark carapace has a reticulate pattern of light lines.

Chicken Turtles occur at Virginia Beach and in the coastal plain of southeastern North Carolina and all of South Carolina. They inhabit quiet water, avoiding rivers, and are especially partial to ponds and ditches in pine savannas. They wander extensively overland.

Nesting is prolonged, beginning in mid-March in South Carolina. Five to 15 eggs are laid at a time, and there are probably several complements in a season. The young grow 25 to 30 mm a year until maturity—about 100 mm for males, 150 mm for females. The young are mostly carnivorous, but adults also eat plants.

**Map Turtle** *Graptemys geographica*

Males 100 to 160 mm (4 to 6 in.), females 175 to 270 mm (7 to 10.5 in.) Map Turtles are olive green to brownish with narrow yellow stripes on the head and limbs and yellow reticulations on the shell. The plastron is yellow and unmarked in the adult. The carapace has a low but distinct keel and is strongly serrate posteriorly. The crushing surfaces of the jaws are broad and smooth. Similar species of *Chrysemys* lack a distinct median keel in the adult, and the crushing surfaces of the jaws are ridged or toothed. The female is larger and has a broader head and heavier jaws than the male.

The Map Turtle enters our area only through the Tennessee River system in extreme western Virginia. It prefers large waters without strong currents. It often basks on logs and snags, but is wary and hard to approach. The massive jaws of females are well adapted to crushing their favorite food—mollusks and crayfish. The males probably eat more insects. In early summer, a female lays 10 to 16 eggs in a flask-shaped hole.

**Diamondback Terrapin** *Malaclemys terrapin*

Males 100 to 140 mm (4 to 5.5 in.), females 150 to 230 mm (6 to 9 in.)
This usually dull-colored turtle has a gray, brown, or black carapace and a lighter plastron of greenish to yellow. The skin of the
neck and legs may be grayish with black spots or linear flecks, or
completely dark. The individual scutes have prominent concentric
age rings which may be worn smooth in old specimens.

   This salt-marsh turtle is found in the tidal channels of our
sounds and estuaries that are bordered chiefly by *Spartina*.

   The Diamondback was the epicure's delight almost a century
ago when it sold for nearly a dollar an inch to provide soup for
the table. Populations were severely depleted before a slumping
market and changing tastes per-
mitted a marked recovery. Com-
mercial collection at present is
localized.

   A female seeks a suitable site
above high tide and deposits a
complement of 4 to 12 eggs, averaging about 30 mm long. She may
lay several clutches per season beginning in May or June. Maximum
egg production occurs at about
25 years of age.

**Eastern Box Turtle** *Terrapene carolina*

114 to 165 mm (4.5 to 6.5 in.) This well-known turtle has a brown, dome-shaped carapace, variously mottled with yellow or orange, and a hinged plastron that allows the turtle to withdraw and enclose its head, limbs, and tail within the shell. Adult males have concave plastrons and often red eyes; adult females have flat plastrons and brown or yellow eyes.

This species lives in forested habitats throughout the area up to about 1,220 m elevation.

These turtles are largely terrestrial, but they often enter water during hot, dry weather. In the early morning and after rains, individuals frequently wander across roads where many are killed by cars. Box Turtles eat a wide variety of plants and small animals. Several kinds of poisonous mushrooms are included in their diet, and cases of poisoning are known in some persons who have eaten these reptiles. A female lays from three to eight eggs, usually in June or July, and hatching occurs in about 3 months. The hatchlings are about 30 mm in carapace length.

**Gopher Tortoise** *Gopherus polyphemus*

150 to 368 mm (6 to 14.5 in.) This large turtle has a high, dorsally flattened brown or tan carapace. The carapacial scutes have light centers, which are yellow or orange in the young. The unhinged dull yellow plastron bears a large gular projection, a feature not present in other turtles of the area. The head, legs, and tail are brown or gray. The front legs are shovellike and heavily scaled; the hind ones are elephantine.

Gopher Turtles live in rolling sandhill areas characterized by wide patches of white sand, scattered clumps of wire grass, turkey oak, and longleaf pine. This rare species is known in the area only from Jasper and Hampton counties, South Carolina.

This turtle excavates an extensive burrow up to 10 m long; the entrance is usually marked by a small mound of sand. It is diurnal and feeds mainly on grasses and fruits. In late spring or early summer, females deposit four to seven spherical eggs in nests usually located far from the burrow. Various other animals may occupy the burrows, including Crawfish Frogs and Diamondback Rattlesnakes.

*Photograph by Peter C. H. Pritchard*

*Photograph by Peter C. H. Pritchard*

**Leatherback** *Dermochelys coriacea*

1,180 to 1,780 mm (46 to 70 in.); 295 to 680 kg (650 to 1,500 lbs.)
Instead of horny scutes, this monster among turtles has a shell of
leathery skin covering a mosaic of small irregular bones. Its cara-

pace has seven longitudinal ridges, its plastron five. There are no claws on the flippers. The color is dark brown or black, sometimes with light blotches on the head, neck, and flippers, especially in the young. The neck is short and not as retractile as in other sea turtles.

Although primarily tropical, the Leatherback wanders farther north than other sea turtles and may reach Nova Scotia and New-foundland. It is capable of maintaining a deep body temperature far above that of the water, apparently through muscular activity and fatty insulation. This powerful swimmer is the most pelagic of all turtles. Leatherbacks are omnivorous, eating sea urchins, crustaceans, fish, mollusks, and plants, but their favorite food appears to be jellyfish, including the Portuguese man-of-war.

The Leatherback nests at night on widely scattered tropical beaches, often sharing them with other species of marine turtles. There is one nesting record from Cape Lookout, North Carolina. A female will lay several times a season at about 10-day intervals, but probably not every year. Usually about one-third of the 50 to 170 eggs laid are yolkless.

This species is everywhere rare. One authority estimated the world population of females at 1,000, but that is probably too low. As with all sea turtles, the eggs are edible and the nests are often raided by man and other predators. The flesh, however, is nowhere esteemed, but it does provide an oil used commercially as a base for many cosmetics.

## Loggerhead *Caretta caretta*

800 to 1,200 mm (31 to 47 in.); 77 to 227 kg (170 to 500 lbs.) This is the sea turtle most often seen on our coast. It is very large, has a massive head, and is the only reddish brown species. The nuchal scute contacts the first of five pairs of pleural scutes, and usually three scutes on a side form the bridge between the carapace and plastron.

The Loggerhead is basically tropical and subtropical but has been recorded from Argentina to Newfoundland and the British Isles. These animals are great wanderers, and tagged individuals have been taken well over 1,600 km from the point of marking. They are omnivorous feeders.

This turtle nests sparingly at least as far north as Ocracoke Inlet (formerly to Virginia) and commonly in South Carolina. Like most sea turtles, they nest on isolated beaches in late spring and early summer. Mating occurs just beyond the surf. At night the female crawls ashore and selects a suitable site for her nest, usually along the dune front. With her hind flippers, she excavates an egg chamber 15 to 25 cm in diameter and 12 to 50 cm below the surface. Into this she lays from 64 to 341 eggs. She then covers the nest by scraping sand and crawling over it until the precise location is obscured. An individual lays on a 2- or 3-year cycle but will deposit two to six clutches at about 2-week intervals in her nesting year. The young emerge at night about 2 months later and make their way to the sea. Illumination, slope of the beach, and the white surf probably are directional cues to the young.

**Green Turtle** *Chelonia mydas*

760 to 1,530 mm (30 to 60 in.); 100 to 295 kg (220 to 650 lbs.) This large sea turtle is distinguished from the others by a single pair of elongate scales between the eyes, a strongly serrate lower jaw, and a single claw on each front flipper. The Green Turtle and the Hawksbill have four instead of five pairs of pleural scutes.

Green Turtles are pan-tropical in distribution. They readily migrate long distances across open seas but spend most time in shallow waters feeding mainly on eel grass (*Zostera*), mangrove, turtle grass (*Thallasia*), and other plants. In our area, this turtle is a rare straggler. It does not nest here.

Unlike other sea turtles, this species occasionally comes ashore to bask. The Green Turtle is well adapted for prolonged diving; it can survive up to 5 hours with no detectable oxygen in its blood and with 9-minute intervals between heart beats.

The common name is derived from the color of the body fat, which lends to its meat an exquisite flavor. The Green Turtle has been termed the most valuable reptile in the world. It occurs in large numbers in the Caribbean region; however, many breeding colonies have been greatly reduced, and some have been exterminated. Because its eggs and flesh are eagerly sought, the future for this species is dim. Nesting colonies are finally being protected, and the weaker ones are receiving egg transplants. The intensive studies of reproduction and migration that are underway should provide a basis for sustained management. Adequate international cooperation must be realized.

*Photograph by Peter C. H. Pritchard*

## Hawksbill *Eretmochelys imbricata*

750 to 915 mm (29.5 to 36 in.); 36.5 to 127 kg (80 to 280 lbs.) The large scutes of the carapace of this small sea turtle overlap (except in the very young and old), hence, the specific name. The head is relatively small with a narrow snout and smooth cutting edges on the jaws, suggesting a hawk's bill. The carapace, like that of the Green Turtle, has four pairs of pleural scutes, the first of which does not contact the nuchal. The Hawksbill has two pairs of scales between the eyes and nostrils, unlike the Green Turtle, which has but one pair.

The Hawksbill inhabits tropical seas and only rarely wanders to our shores. It prefers coral reefs and rocky ledges where it forages for a wide variety of sessile and sluggish invertebrates. It also consumes algae, mangroves, and many other types of plants.

A Hawksbill is very aggressive when molested and can inflict painful bites. Because this turtle is the source of tortoiseshell, a product used in many ornamental articles, it has been widely exploited and now is an endangered species. For a time, modern plastics alleviated the pressures on this turtle, but the demand for genuine tortoiseshell has returned and with it a gloomy forecast for the Hawksbill.

Hawksbills nest earlier and have more diffuse breeding patterns than the highly gregarious Green Turtle. This behavior makes

*Photograph by Peter C. H. Pritchard*

them and their nests more difficult to protect against predation. Females probably nest every 2 or 3 years and lay two or more clutches of about 160 eggs at about 2-week intervals. Mating occurs immediately after a spent female returns to the sea. Like the other marine turtles, little is known about the young once they enter the sea.

*Photograph by Peter C. H. Pritchard*

**Ridley** *Lepidochelys kempi*

580 to 750 mm (23 to 30 in.); 36 to 50 kg (79 to 110 lbs.) This is the smallest of our sea turtles. Its heart-shaped carapace is about as broad as it is long. Among sea turtles the Ridley is unique in its gray coloration and in having a secretory pore near the posterior edge of each scute forming the bridge. The nuchal scute contacts the first of five pairs of pleural scutes as in the Loggerhead.

The Ridley inhabits the Gulf of Mexico and the East Coast, straying to Nova Scotia and Europe. It is uncommon along our shores. This turtle feeds largely on crabs and mollusks, but it also eats other invertebrates and plants. Captives are nervous and bad tempered.

The Ridley differs from other sea turtles in the remarkable concentration of breeding effort that takes place in the daytime. Immense groups, called *arribadas*, of as many as 40,000 females come ashore on a stretch of beach about 2 km long in Tampico, Mexico, on a single day. There may be 10,000 ashore at once during the 4 to 6 hours required to complete nesting. There are usually three such *arribadas* in a year, at slightly different sites, about 10 days apart, between late March and the end of June. As many as 180 eggs per clutch are laid in the first nesting, and as few as 80 in the third. Coyotes gather at these times in great numbers and destroy most eggs. Vultures and voracious fish account for the

*Photograph by Peter C. H. Pritchard*

disappearance of many hatchlings. Man of course is a major predator on both eggs and adults.

This remarkable breeding pattern and its site were discovered less than 20 years ago. It is hoped that the concentration of nesting will lend itself to effective conservation strategy, but at present the Ridley is one of the most imperiled reptiles in the world.

## Florida Softshell *Trionyx ferox*

Males 150 to 292 mm (6 to 11 in.), females 200 to 498 mm (8 to 19.5 in.) This pancake-shaped turtle has a very long neck, a narrow head with a slender, snorkellike snout, and a soft leathery shell that lacks horny scutes. The dark brown to brownish gray carapace has a distinct marginal ridge; small hemispherical anterior projections; and in some individuals, large, obscure dark spots. The feet are extensively webbed. Spiny Softshells lack both the carapacial projections and the ridge. These turtles should not be handled; their sharp claws and jaws are especially dangerous.

In our area, the Florida Softshell lives in rivers, ponds, and lakes only in the Combahee and Savannah river systems in southern South Carolina.

Females deposit 10 to 22 eggs in early summer in sunlit, sandy areas on the banks of rivers. Incubation requires about 2½ months. This turtle is omnivorous, but prefers crayfish, mollusks, frogs, and fish.

**Spiny Softshell** *Trionyx spiniferus*

Males 125 to 235 mm (5 to 9 in.), females 180 to 450 mm (7 to 18 in.)
The leathery carapace and tubular nostrils of softshells are so distinctive that they cannot be confused with any hardshell turtle.
This species differs from the Florida Softshell by having spines on
the front edge of the carapace and by having strongly patterned
feet. Juveniles and males have sharp black spots, or ocelli, on the
back; adult females, indistinct blotches. The large nostrils have a
ridge on each median side.

This species occurs in the Clinch and Holston systems in southwestern Virginia and the French Broad River of North Carolina. In
the Atlantic drainage, it has been found in all systems south and
west of Cape Fear.

These turtles occur in large
streams with sandy bottoms and
in ponds and lakes. They often
bury themselves in shallow water
and extend their long necks to
permit the terminal nostrils to
break the surface for breathing.
The eggs are nearly spherical and
about 22 mm in diameter. They are
deposited 10 to 25 cm deep in
sandy banks.

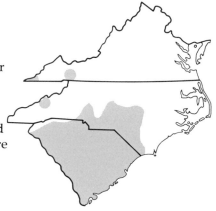

## Order Squamata

LIZARDS AND SNAKES

The Squamata are the most numerous of living reptiles. They originated in the early Mesozoic from lizardlike Eosuchia and radiated in late Mesozoic and Cenozoic times. They have many salient traits: (1) The lower jaw joins a movable bone, the quadrate, which in turn articulates with the skull. (2) The roof of the mouth bears an interesting chemoreceptor, Jacobson's organ. It also occurs in amphibians and some mammals but occurs only in the embryos of other reptiles. Snakes and many lizards often flick their long, narrow tongues out of the mouth, then insert the tips into Jacobson's organ, which detects odorous particles adhering to the tongue. (3) The cloacal opening is a transverse slit, rather than a longitudinal one as in other living reptiles. (4) This transverse opening is, in part, an adaptation for the unusual paired copulatory organs known as hemipenes. Either hemipenis can become engorged with blood and everted into the cloaca of the female. (5) The Squamata produce large eggs but, unlike other reptiles, their eggs lack albumin. Most are oviparous: some species retain the eggs in the distal part of the oviduct and lay them shortly before hatching; others retain the eggs until they hatch, and the young are born alive. Those species in which hatching coincides with birth are termed *ovoviviparous*. In many live-bearing species, the metabolic exchange between the female and her young is completely respiratory, but in some there is a nutritional exchange as well. Most species living at high latitudes or high altitudes are ovoviviparous. (6) Emergence of the young squamata from the egg is made easy by an "egg tooth." This true tooth erupts from the upper gum shortly before hatching, projects under the lip, and cuts the egg membrane or shell as the young moves its head about. An egg tooth also occurs in ovoviviparous species, and it too is lost about the time of birth. The egg tooth differs greatly from the broad, cornified "egg caruncle" of other reptiles, the birds, and the egg-laying mammals.

## Suborder Sauria = Lacertilia

LIZARDS

This is the most successful group of living reptiles; about 3,000 species are known. Most lizards have four legs with five toes on each foot, but some (especially the burrowing forms) have lost toes and even legs. In contrast to snakes, lizards have movable eyelids and a middle ear, a tympanum, and an ear canal. The quadrate bone is only slightly movable, and the right and left halves of the lower jaw are firmly united, thus restricting the size of the mouth opening and the size of prey eaten. The tail of many lizards is easily broken and soon regenerates. Many have an armor of bony scutes (osteoderms) in the dermal layer of the skin. Adults of our native species range in total length from 80 mm (Ground Skink) to 1,180 mm (Slender Glass Lizard).

Lizards have undergone extensive adaptive radiation and have invaded a wide variety of habitats. Some are highly aquatic and others are well adapted to life in the desert. Most are carnivores, but a few are vegetarians.

In spite of the great diversity and wide distribution of lizards, our fauna is strikingly impoverished. Only 12 species occur in the area, and one of these, the Horned Lizard, has been introduced and is restricted to a few coastal islands in South Carolina. As might be expected, the warmest part of our area, the coastal plain of South Carolina, has the most species (11) and the mountains of Virginia, the fewest (6). Only 3 species occur throughout the area. Most native species are skinks (5), or glass lizards (3). None of our lizards is venomous, and all lay eggs and feed mainly on insects.

**Carolina Anole** *Anolis carolinensis*

130 to 200 mm (5 to 8 in.) This arboreal lizard is familiar to everyone spending much time outdoors in the coastal plain of the Carolinas. In bright light on a green background, an anole is usually a light emerald green, but in damp, cool, or dark situations, a dull olive, brown or gray color appears. A defending or courting male is green with a bright pink dewlap, or throat fan. The causative factors behind these color changes are complex. No other lizard in our area can undergo such color changes. Many species of anoles occur in the American tropics.

The Carolina Anole ranges throughout the coastal plain and southern piedmont of North Carolina and all of South Carolina. It is common in disturbed areas such as roadsides, forest edges, and old building sites having an abundance of shrubbery and sunlight.

The reproductive biology of this species has been studied intensely. The gonads are regulated primarily by photoperiod. They enlarge during the warm, lengthening days of spring and regress with the shortening days of late summer. The male is strongly territorial. When approached by another male, he compresses his body, extends his throat fan, and bobs his head. If the intruder continues to approach, aggressive fighting ensues. Although a male's territory is relatively small, about 1 m³, it often encompasses the home ranges of two or three females. As in the human

female, only one ovarian follicle develops at a time, and the ovaries alternate in egg production. A female anole is capable of producing one egg every 2 weeks for the entire breeding season, but before producing each egg she must be courted. The sight of a displaying

male triggers ovarian development, which, in turn, evokes sexual receptivity, and later, ovulation. The female may store viable sperm for at least 8 months after copulation. The egg is soft-shelled and laid in a shallow depression in moist soil, leaf litter, rotten wood, or a hole in a tree. It hatches in 7 weeks and the hatchling is 55 to 60 mm long. Small insects and spiders are the primary food.

**Texas Horned Lizard** *Phrynosoma cornutum*

60 to 181 mm (2.5 to 7 in.) Texas Horned Lizards, erroneously called horned toads, have dorsoventrally flattened light brown or gray bodies. The back is covered with short spines and prominent dark spots. A two-rowed fringe of triangular scales borders each side. Two stout spines on the top of the head project upward.

The native range of this introduced species includes Texas, Oklahoma, most of Kansas, and portions of adjoining states. Established populations occur in South Carolina on two barrier islands near Charleston and on the beachfront near Murrell's Inlet. These colonies occupy open grassy or sandy areas behind the primary dunes.

Horned Lizards are active mainly during the summer and feed largely on ants. In the western United States, females deposit 23 to 37 eggs in a pocket of sand about 15 cm deep; these require 39 to 47 days to hatch. Members of this species can eject blood from the corners of their eyes to a distance of a few meters. The function of this bizarre habit is not understood.

**Eastern Fence Lizard** *Sceloporus undulatus*

100 to 184 mm (4 to 7 in.) The Fence Lizard is gray or brown above with indistinct darker markings. Mature males have a bright greenish blue area bordered medially with black on each side of the belly. Conspicuous keeled scales give a rough appearance.

This abundant lizard occurs throughout most of our area. It inhabits open situations with plenty of sunlight such as building sites, slab piles, open pine woods, fences, and rocky places. It avoids dense woods, is scarce at high elevations, and is absent from the outer banks.

Emergence from hibernation occurs with warm sunny weather in March. Courting males are territorial and defend against rival males by bobbing their heads and standing high to display their bright belly colors. A female lays from 6 to 10 eggs in late spring in burrows under rotten logs, sawdust piles, or similar places, and hatching takes place in mid-summer. She may produce a second clutch in an extended season. Food includes beetles, grass-hoppers, caterpillars, spiders, and snails.

**Coal Skink** *Eumeces anthracinus*

130 to 178 mm (5 to 7 in.) This small skink has four dorsal light stripes, whereas other *Eumeces* have five or seven. The light dorsal head stripes of other skinks (except older adults) are also absent. Coal Skinks have one postmental scale; other skinks have two. Adults are olive gray to olive brown above, and bluish or gray below. Virginia Coal Skinks have a light stripe through the posterior upper labials; the blue-tailed young otherwise resemble the adults. Carolina Coal Skinks have light spots on the centers of these scales, and the blue-tailed young have black bodies.

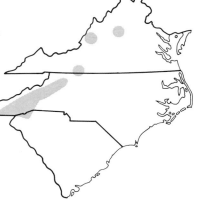

Coal Skinks live under logs, rocks, or leaf litter on wooded, rocky hillsides, usually near water. Widely disjunct populations are known in the area from the mountains of Virginia, North Carolina, and Sassafras Mountain, South Carolina.

This lizard is uncommon and secretive. It readily enters water when pursued, but its habits are generally similar to those of other skinks.

*Five-lined Skink (adult female)*

## Five-lined Skink *Eumeces fasciatus*

130 to 205 mm (5 to 8 in.) The three species of large blue-tailed skinks (*Eumeces*) are difficult to distinguish, especially in the field. The tail is brownish in adults but brilliant blue in juveniles. This species has five light stripes on a dark background, whereas the other two species in our area usually have seven. In large males, the stripes are lost, and the head is coppery red throughout the breeding season. The lateral dark stripe of the tail is longest in this species, extending more than half the length of the tail. The Five-lined Skink is slightly smaller than the Southeastern Five-lined Skink, and its median subcaudal scale row is wider than the adjacent rows. It is considerably smaller than the Broadhead Skink, averages two fewer rows of scales around the body (28 to 30), and usually has four instead of five scales on the upper lip before the subocular scale.

This species is absent in our area only from the outer banks and the higher elevations in the mountains. Its total range corresponds closely with the eastern deciduous forest. Although it likes to bask in sunlight on logs, fences, rocks, and footbridges, it prefers a more mesic habitat than the other large skinks.

Skinks do not defend defined areas; hence, they are not truly territorial, but during the mating season in April and May, males

*Five-lined Skink (juvenile)*

are hostile to each other, and chance encounters result in physical combat, sometimes with serious injury.

In rotten wood or under a rock, a female lays about 6 to 12 eggs, the number varying with her size. She guards the nest, turning the eggs daily, and will void on them if they become too dry. Eggs are usually laid in June, and hatching occurs about a month later. Sexual maturity is attained in the second spring.

Skinks feed predominantly on arthropods, the choice dependent on the size of the lizard and the availability of prey, with preference for large items such as big spiders, crickets, grasshoppers, beetles, harvestmen, and snails.

**Southeastern Five-lined Skink** *Eumeces inexpectatus*

140 to 216 mm (5.5 to 8.5 in.) This species is best distinguished
from the other blue-tailed skinks by the narrow midventral subcaudal scale row. Near the base of the tail, this row is little if any
wider than the adjacent rows. The dorsolateral stripes are on the
fourth and fifth lateral rows rather than the third and fourth as
in the other species. This and the Broadhead Skink in our area
usually have a pair of sublateral light stripes, seven light stripes in
all. In juveniles, the head stripes and the middorsal stripe usually

do not meet, whereas in the other two species, they converge at the back of the head. The snout and head stripes of hatchlings are orange.

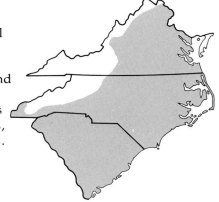

The Southeastern Five-lined Skink is abundant on the coastal plain, but occurs sparingly elsewhere in our area. It is the only large skink on the outer banks and on most coastal islands.

It thrives in disturbed habitats such as recently lumbered lands, old house sites, and beach areas. Its habits are similar to those of the Five-lined Skink, but it is somewhat less arboreal.

**Broadhead Skink** *Eumeces laticeps*

165 to 325 mm (6.5 to 13 in.) This is our largest skink. It has 30 or 32 scale rows around the body and five upper labial scales before the subocular scale. Large males lose all traces of stripes and have a broad head, which is red during the breeding season. Females are smaller and retain at least remnants of the striped pattern common to the blue-tailed skinks. This species differs from the Southeastern Five-lined Skink by having wide scales in the middle row under the tail. Its young differ from those of the Five-lined Skink by being larger and usually having seven light stripes and longer toes and claws.

The Broadhead Skink inhabits all of our area except the higher mountains and the outer banks. It occurs on some barrier islands in South Carolina, and is most abundant on some of the coastal estates and old plantations where it finds its favorite habitat—large spreading trees such as live oak, water oak, and cypress. It is very arboreal and frequents living and dead trees to considerable heights. Throughout its range it prefers warmer and more xeric habitats than does the Five-lined Skink.

Skinks maintain their body temperature at favorable levels by basking in the sun when cool and seeking shade when warm. They prefer temperatures a few degrees below those of several other lizards and may be active in early spring before other species appear.

Skinks are known as "scorpions" to many rural folk who consider them venomous. Because of its size, the Broadhead Skink figures most prominently in these notions, and a large one is capable of giving a painful but harmless nip to the unwary collector.

The 6 to 15 eggs, laid in June or July, usually hatch by September. Hatchlings are about 70 mm long. The habits of the Broadhead Skink are similar to those of the Five-lined Skink; however, by being more arboreal, it sometimes nests in cavities in trees, and it has a somewhat different choice of food items. The comparative ecology and behavior of our three large sympatric skinks is a challenging subject for study.

**Ground Skink** *Scincella lateralis*

80 to 130 mm (3 to 5 in.) This diminutive skink is our smallest
lizard. It is brownish and shiny with a dark dorsolateral stripe, the
lower edge of which is ill defined and blends into the whitish or
yellow belly. This lizard may be mistaken at a glance for a Dwarf or
Two-lined Salamander.

This species is common except in the mountains, where it is
absent or local. Its nearest relatives are found in Central America
and the Orient. In disturbed areas and open woodlands, particularly those with pine, it is more often heard than seen as it scurries
off in the leaf litter. True to its name, it lives close to the surface and
needs little cover to hide effectively. Activity is greatest during
warm humid weather.

A female lays from one to seven
eggs per clutch depending on her
size. An egg is about 9 mm long,
and development is well under
way when laid. Two or more
clutches may be laid in a season,
and early broods mature within
the year. This is a short-lived
species; about 10 percent survive 2
years and few, if any, a 4th year.

## Six-lined Racerunner *Cnemidophorus sexlineatus*

150 to 240 mm (6 to 9.5 in.) The Racerunner has six whitish to yellow stripes on a dark background. The dorsal scales are tiny granules, but the belly scales are large, quadrangular, and in eight regular rows. The tail is long and slim and is brownish or gray in the adult, but bluish in the young. Racerunners resemble the skinks, which, however, are shiny and have bright blue tails as juveniles.

Racerunners occur from the outer banks to the mountains but avoid elevations above about 650 m. These alert inhabitants of open, usually sandy areas can quickly take cover under clumps of grass or in underground burrows. In warm weather they are most difficult to catch by hand.

Egg number depends on the size of the female, with five to six maximum. The eggs are laid a few centimeters under the surface; sawdust piles are favorite nesting sites. The nesting season is prolonged, and older females lay two clutches per season. The hatchlings appear from late June into September.

### Slender Glass Lizard *Ophisaurus attenuatus*

559 to 1,180 mm (22 to 46.5 in.) Glass Lizards are legless and closely resemble snakes, but have movable eyelids, external ear openings, and a groove along each side of the body. The Slender Glass Lizard has dark lines below the lateral groove and often under the tail. The back is brown or tan, usually with a dark median stripe or a trace of one. Along each side are several black stripes and thin white or yellowish lines. Some large adults have pale dorsal cross-bars with dark margins. The long fragile tail is often broken, and the regenerated tip is light-colored.

This species occurs in eastern Virginia, much of North Carolina, and all of South Carolina. It apparently is absent from most of the mountains. Favorite habitats are grassy fields, woodland margins, and other open, usually dry places.

Slender Glass Lizards are extremely energetic. They thrash about when handled and are difficult to catch without breaking the tail. These reptiles eat invertebrates, small lizards and snakes, and the eggs of ground-nesting birds. A female lays from 4 to 19 eggs per clutch; hatchlings are about 185 mm long.

**Island Glass Lizard** *Ophisaurus compressus*

380 to 610 mm (15 to 24 in.) This glass lizard has one dark stripe on each side of the body through the third and fourth scale rows above the lateral groove. The back is usually unpatterned, but a median dark stripe is sometimes present; this may be broken into short segments. Small white spots, generally one at the edge of each scale, mark the body anteriorly, and distinct white bars are usually present on the neck. Unlike our other glass lizards, there are no scales between the upper labials and the eye.

Island Glass Lizards prefer xeric habitats in coastal pine and maritime forests. They are found occasionally under tidal wrack on sandy beaches. This rare species is known in our area only in Charleston, Georgetown, and Jasper counties, South Carolina.

The biology of this glass lizard is poorly known. Hatchlings are smaller than those of other species. The caudal vertebrae lack fracture planes, hence the tail is less easily broken than in related species.

### Eastern Glass Lizard *Ophisaurus ventralis*

457 to 1,067 mm (18 to 42 in.) This large legless lizard differs from the Slender Glass Lizard by lacking dark marks below the lateral groove, and from the Island Glass Lizard by having small scales between the eye and upper labials. The dorsal color is usually brown or tan, and one or more dark stripes occur along each side of the body. Most large adults are greenish.

This species ranges throughout the coastal plain of South Carolina and in most of eastern North Carolina. Favorite habitats are flatwoods, maritime forests, and other sandy environments. These lizards frequently are abundant under rubbish in fields and vacant lots near ponds, marshes, and estuaries.

Individuals forage chiefly in the early morning and late afternoon but are sometimes active at night. In late spring or summer, a female Eastern Glass Lizard deposits from 5 to 17 eggs, usually in a shallow depression under a log or similar object, and she often remains with the eggs until they hatch. The hatchling is about 185 mm long.

## Suborder Serpentes = Ophidia

SNAKES

The earliest known snakes date from the late Cretaceous, about 80 million years ago. They unquestionably evolved from lizards, but fossil verification is still lacking. Unlike most lizards, snakes lack legs; however, some primitive families retain traces of the pelvic girdle, and a few have traces of legs. All lack movable eyelids, a middle ear, and osteoderms (bones in the skin). Snakes have extremely long vertebral columns, containing as many as 440 vertebrae. Adults range in size from 100 mm to about 10 m. Snakes cannot break off and regenerate the tail, as many lizards do. If the tail is broken, a snake remains stub tailed for the remainder of its life.

All snakes are carnivores. Many swallow their prey alive, but some first wrap their body tightly around a prey and suffocate it. Others have salivary glands specialized to produce poisons and tubular teeth to inject the poison, thus immobilizing the prey. Snakes do not chew their food; they swallow organisms whole. Their needlelike teeth simply prevent prey from escaping. The jaw mechanism is usually flexible. The quadrate bone is highly movable, and the right and left halves of the lower jaw are united by an elastic ligament, thus permitting large animals to be swallowed. Snakes contribute greatly to man's well-being by controlling destructive pests, chiefly rats and mice.

This highly successful group comprises 13 families, 396 genera, and about 2,700 species. In addition to burrowing in sand, soil, or mud, they are well adapted to life in fresh water, the open ocean, in trees, and on the ground. The majority of species inhabit the tropics but many abound in the temperate zone. Most snakes (270 of the 396 genera) are in the cosmopolitan family Colubridae, an enigmatic and complex assemblage.

Our area has a rich fauna containing 39 species, 33 of which are colubrids. *Nerodia* (Water Snakes) with 5 species is the largest genus, *Lampropeltis* (Kingsnakes) with 3 is next, 10 genera have 2 species each, and 11 genera are monotypic. Eleven species occur areawide and none is endemic or even closely endemic. The coastal plain of the Carolinas has the most species (37) and the mountains of Virginia, the fewest (22). Six of our species (3 Rattlesnakes, Copperhead, Cottonmouth, and Coral Snake) are highly venomous. Most species mate in April or May and the young appear in August or September. About half of our species are ovoviviparous.

The treatment and management of venomous snakebite, one of the most controversial issues in clinical medicine today, is beyond the scope of this book. Several of the better recent references about this topic are: S. A. Minton, Jr., *Venom Diseases* (Charles C. Thomas Publishers, 1974); F. E. Russell et al., *Journal of the American Medical Association* 233(1975):341–44; W. A. Wingert and J. Wainschel, *Southern Medical Journal* 68(1975):1015–26; and M. S. Sabback et al., *Journal of Trauma* 17(1977):569–74.

**Worm Snake** *Carphophis amoenus*

191 to 318 mm (7.5 to 12.5 in.) Among the smallest of North American serpents, this species is characterized by its small, pointed head, plain chestnut to dark brown dorsum, and pinkish, translucent venter. Its tail tip bears a sharp but completely harmless spine. Dorsal scales are smooth and glossy. These snakes are appropriately named for they indeed resemble large worms.

This species occurs in forested places, especially in moist environments, throughout Virginia and the Carolinas up to about 1,300 m elevation.

Worm Snakes are highly secretive, spending most of the day beneath stones, logs, and other cover and prowling on the surface chiefly at night. They are excellent burrowers, and individuals are sometimes uncovered during excavation or gardening. Worm Snakes are inoffensive and do not bite. Earthworms constitute the principal food. A female deposits from two to eight eggs per clutch, frequently in old sawdust piles or rotten logs. Hatchlings are about 100 mm long and are usually darker than the adults.

**Scarlet Snake** *Cemophora coccinea*

356 to 660 mm (14 to 26 in.) These small, smooth-scaled snakes are brightly marked with red blotches enclosed in black margins and separated by white, yellow, or pale gray interspaces. The under-surface is white, translucent, and glossy. The red snout projects well beyond the lower jaw.

Scarlet Snakes inhabit the coastal plain and piedmont but are absent from most of the mountains. Although their habitats are varied, these snakes are most common in the sandhills and sandy pine flatwoods of the Carolina coastal plain.

Scarlet Snakes are adept burrowers, spending daylight hours underground and prowling on the surface usually at night when they may be found on roads. Most individuals do not bite, even when first handled. Insects, lizards, small snakes, newborn mice, and especially reptile eggs constitute the diet. An active prey is re-strained by constriction. The eggs per clutch vary from two to six, and hatchlings are about 130 mm long. Much remains to be learned about this secretive snake in our area.

*Black Racer (adult)*

**Black Racer** *Coluber constrictor*

BIG

914 to 1,676 mm (36 to 66 in.) Adults of this abundant and well-known snake have a uniformly black dorsum and a predominately black or dark gray undersurface. The chin and sometimes the anterior venter is variously mottled with white. Juveniles have conspicuous brown, gray, or reddish dorsal blotches on a paler ground color. The dorsal scales are smooth.

Black Racers occur throughout the area up to about 1,400 m elevation. In the mountains, they are most common in valleys and at lower altitudes. Habitats range from brushy dunes and maritime forests to rocky hillsides and upland meadows. Individuals frequently hide beneath boards, pieces of tin, and other surface cover around rural buildings and old sawdust piles.

This strictly diurnal species is among the most agile of our snakes. When surprised, most Black Racers crawl rapidly away, disappearing down a nearby hole or into thick vegetation. If cornered or restrained, they vibrate the tail and actively defend themselves, sometimes making wild lunges at the intruder. However, their small teeth, like those of most other nonvenomous snakes, inflict only superficial cuts similar to those resulting from briar scratches. Most ordinary clothing provides more than adequate protection against the bites of these and other nonvenomous snakes in the region. Insects, amphibians, reptiles, birds and their

*Black Racer (juvenile)*

eggs, and small mammals constitute the principal food. Most Black Racers mate in the spring, and in June or July a female lays from 4 to 25 eggs that vary considerably in size and shape. Numerous small nodules on the shells give the appearance that the eggs have been sprinkled with salt. Like many snakes, Racers deposit their eggs under stones and in sawdust piles, rotten logs and stumps, and similar places. Several nests have been exposed by a plow in sandy fields. Hatchlings emerge in late summer or early fall and are about 290 mm long.

**Ringneck Snake** *Diadophis punctatus*

254 to 508 mm (10 to 20 in.) Easily identified by its bright yellow or orange collar, the Ringneck Snake in our area is a small black or slate gray species with smooth scales and a yellow or orange undersurface. In most of South Carolina and the coastal plain of North Carolina and Virginia, Ringneck Snakes have incomplete neck rings, a prominent row of black spots down the center of the belly, small black spots on the chin and some of the lower labials, seven upper labials per side, and fewer than 190 ventrals plus subcaudals. Individuals from northern and western Virginia and from most of the Carolina mountains usually have a complete neck ring, eight upper labials per side, and more than 190 ventrals plus subcaudals. Belly, chin, and lower labial spotting is generally weak or absent. The largest Ringneck Snakes occur in the mountains.

This species, common and widespread in most of the United States, ranges throughout the area below about 1,750 m elevation. Ringneck Snakes frequent forested habitats and are most often found beneath stones and in or under decaying logs and stumps, especially in moist places. Surface activity occurs chiefly at night, when individuals are sometimes found on roads.

Specimens, when first captured, discharge musk and thrash about vigorously, but Ringneck Snakes rarely attempt to bite.

Earthworms and small salamanders constitute the principal food, but these serpents also eat frogs, lizards, and small snakes. A female deposits from 1 to 10 eggs per clutch in old sawdust piles, rotten logs, or in damp soil under flat stones. Like many snakes, the largest females lay the most eggs. Seven hatchlings from the coastal plain of North Carolina averaged 108 mm in length, and 77 hatchlings from the North Carolina mountains averaged 130 mm in length.

## Corn Snake *Elaphe guttata* Big

762 to 1,829 mm (30 to 72 in.) This beautiful snake is red, gray, orange, or brown with prominent reddish brown blotches outlined with black. The venter is boldly checkered with black and white. There is a dark mark on top of the head that resembles a spear point. The dorsal scales usually have weak keels.

These snakes range over most of the area below about 760 m elevation, but they are most common in pine and wire grass flatwoods and sandhills of the Carolina coastal plain.

Corn Snakes are secretive and frequently hide beneath surface cover, in stump holes, and in burrows of other animals. They climb with ease but are found most often on the ground, and many are unfortunately killed by cars. Recently captured specimens usually bite, but most soon become docile and, with proper care, often thrive in captivity. This powerful constrictor feeds mostly on small mammals. It also eats birds and their eggs, and frogs and lizards are a favorite food of juveniles. A female deposits from 3 to 27 eggs per clutch, and hatchlings are about 320 mm long.

**Rat Snake** *Elaphe obsoleta* *Big*

1,067 to 2,159 mm (42 to 85 in.) This highly variable species is one
of our largest and most abundant snakes. In most of the area, Rat
Snakes have a black or dark brown dorsum and a venter mottled
with gray and white. The anterior portion of the undersurface
is lighter than the posterior portion. Individuals in much of the

*Rat Snake (juvenile)*

coastal plain of the Carolinas are greenish or yellowish with four prominent dark brown or black longitudinal stripes and generally weak and diffuse ventral markings. Juveniles have conspicuous gray or brown blotches on a lighter ground color, and some adults have traces of the blotched pattern. The dorsal scales are weakly keeled.

Rat Snakes range throughout Virginia and the Carolinas up to 1,350 m elevation. Favorite habitats include upland hardwood forests, pocosins, river swamps and lowlands, fields, and barns and other buildings. Juveniles especially sometimes enter inhabited rural dwellings. These snakes are excellent climbers and frequently live in tree hollows, sometimes a considerable distance above the ground.

When approached, a Rat Snake often kinks its body and remains motionless. If provoked, it quickly assumes a defensive posture, vibrates its tail, and strikes. Small mammals and birds and their eggs are the principal food of these large and powerful constrictors, but many frogs and lizards are eaten by young snakes. Because rats and mice constitute a major portion of the diet, Rat Snakes are largely beneficial to man. However, on poultry farms and near nesting boxes for other birds, they may become a minor nuisance. The eggs, often laid in a cluster, vary in number from 5 to 25 per clutch and are deposited in late spring or summer. Rotten logs and stumps, compost mounds, and sawdust piles are favorite nesting places. Hatchlings, averaging about 330 mm long, emerge in late summer or fall.

**Mud Snake** *Farancia abacura*   *BIG*

1,016 to 1,854 mm (40 to 73 in.) Mud Snakes are large and moderately stout bodied with smooth, iridescent scales. Dorsal color is
black; the undersurface, usually red or pink but sometimes white,
has prominent black markings. Ventral ground color extends
upward on the sides to form triangular-shaped bars. The lateral
bars of some individuals, especially juveniles, extend as narrow
crosslines across the dorsum.

Mud Snakes occur in the coastal plain and lower piedmont of the
Carolinas and in southeastern Virginia. They are mostly aquatic
and live in cypress swamps, sluggish lowland streams, and similar
places.

When first caught, a Mud Snake thrashes about
and often presses its pointed but completely harmless tail tip against the captor's skin. This defensive behavior, also characteristic of the
Rainbow Snake, probably is the basis
for the "sting-snake" myth of southern folklore. Amphiumas and
Sirens are the chief food. The
eggs of this often prolific species
number from 4 to 104 per clutch,
and hatchlings are about 200 mm
long.

**Rainbow Snake** *Farancia erytrogramma*

914 to 1,676 mm (36 to 66 in.) This appropriately named species is one of the most colorful snakes. Dorsal ground color is blue black with three longitudinal red stripes. The undersurface is mostly red or pink with two or three rows of black spots. Dorsal scales are smooth and iridescent.

Rainbow Snakes range over most of the coastal plain where habitats include rivers, large creeks, cypress swamps, lakes, and fresh and brackish marshes. In Virginia, especially during the spring, these animals have been exposed by plows in sandy fields near water.

These snakes are secretive and chiefly nocturnal, hiding by day among cypress roots or under various debris. When first seized, a Rainbow Snake often presses its harmless tail tip against the hand but it seldom if ever bites. Amphibians are the main food of juveniles, and adults feed largely on eels (*Anguilla*). The eggs, often deposited in sand, number from 20 to 52 per clutch, and neonates are about 200 mm long.

*Eastern Hognose Snake (individual with head and neck spread).*

*Eastern Hognose Snake (profile of black phase specimen)*

## Eastern Hognose Snake *Heterodon platyrhinos*

508 to 1,194 mm (20 to 47 in.) This moderately large, stout-bodied snake has keeled dorsal scales and an upturned snout with a pronounced median keel. Color patterns are highly variable. Usually

*Eastern Hognose Snake (feigning death)*

the dorsum has dark blotches with light interspaces and varies from brown to shades of red, yellow, or orange, but some individuals are plain black or dark gray. This species differs from the Southern Hognose Snake by having the posterior part of the belly usually darker than the undersurface of the tail. It also attains a larger size, has a less upturned snout, and its body is not as stout as that of the Southern Hognose.

Eastern Hognose Snakes range below about 760 m elevation throughout most of the area, especially in habitats having sandy or friable loamy soils. This species is most common in the coastal plain and generally rare in the mountains.

These reptiles are strictly diurnal and, unlike many snakes, are found crawling abroad more often than under sheltering objects. When alarmed, an individual usually flattens its head and neck and hisses loudly. If further provoked, it may gape its mouth, roll over on its back, and feign death. Because of such extraordinary behavior, this snake is often rumored to be dangerously venomous, and such ominous names as "spreading adder," "black adder," and "blowing viper" are firmly entrenched in the vocabulary of many rural persons. Surprisingly, a Hognose Snake almost never bites, even when first handled. Toads are the principal food, but other amphibians, insects, birds, and small mammals are occasionally eaten. A female produces from 4 to 60 eggs per clutch, usually in June or July, and nests have been discovered a few centimeters below the surface in sandy fields. Hatchlings are about 175 mm long.

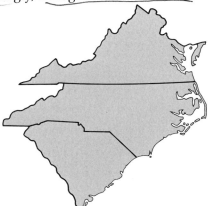

**Southern Hognose Snake** *Heterodon simus*

330 to 559 mm (13 to 22 in.) This small, exceptionally stout-bodied snake has keeled dorsal scales and a prominently upturned snout. Dorsal ground color is brown, tan, or gray with dark blotches and pale interspaces. Unlike the Eastern Hognose Snake, the undersurface of the tail is similar in color to the posterior part of the belly.

Southern Hognose Snakes inhabit the coastal plain of South Carolina and the eastern and southeastern portions of North Carolina. Favorite habitats are sandhills, pine and wire grass flat-woods, and other xeric communities with coarse sands or porous loamy soils.

When disturbed, these snakes hiss and flatten the head and neck, but they seldom bite. Southern Hognose Snakes are effective burrowers. They spend much time underground but are active on the surface during the day, especially in the early morning and late afternoon. Toads are the favorite food, but these snakes sometimes eat other amphibians and occasionally small mammals. A female deposits about 6 to 10 eggs in late spring or summer. Measurements of hatchlings have not been reported.

**Mole Kingsnake** *Lampropeltis calligaster*

762 to 1,168 mm (30 to 46 in.) This moderately large snake has dark blotches on a brown, tan, or reddish dorsum. Juveniles and young adults have bright markings, but some old individuals have very faint ones. The dorsal scales are smooth.

These kingsnakes occur over much of the area, but their distribution in some sections is poorly known. They are absent in most of the mountains, and only a few records are known from the lower coastal plain of South Carolina. Favorite habitats range from sandhills and pine flatwoods to open fields and upland hardwood forests. Although these snakes are accomplished burrowers, they spend much time prowling above ground and under logs and other surface cover. They are also found on roads at night.

When disturbed, a Mole King-snake vibrates its tail and usually attempts to bite. Small mammals, lizards, and snakes are the principal food of these constrictors. A female deposits from 6 to 17 eggs, usually in June or July. Nests have been found a few centimeters below the surface in sandy fields. Hatchlings average about 220 mm long.

### Eastern Kingsnake *Lampropeltis getulus*

914 to 1,753 mm (36 to 69 in.) This large, handsome serpent has smooth, glossy scales. Most Eastern Kingsnakes are black with bright white or yellow chainlike markings. Along the outer banks of North Carolina, from Cape Hatteras to Cape Lookout, these snakes usually are brownish with conspicuous light stippling in the dark areas between the chainlike patterns. In extreme western Virginia, individuals are mostly black with only a faint trace of the chainlike markings.

Eastern Kingsnakes occur below about 760 m elevation in most of the area but they are most common in the coastal plain. They are secretive and often hide under surface cover, especially around sawdust piles and old buildings.

When first caught, a Kingsnake usually expels copious quantities of musk from its cloacal glands, but it soon becomes docile and tolerates handling. These constrictors eat turtle eggs, lizards, birds, small mammals, and other snakes, even venomous ones. The eggs, 5 to 20 per clutch, are laid in rotten logs and similar places. Hatchlings are about 265 mm long.

*Eastern Milk Snake*

*Scarlet Kingsnake*

## Eastern Milk Snake, Scarlet Kingsnake *Lampropeltis triangulum*

This wide-ranging, highly variable species is represented in Virginia and the Carolinas by two subspecies so different that for years they were considered separate species. A zone of inter-

*Scarlet Kingsnake (profile)*

gradation in which snakes have characters intermediate between the Scarlet Kingsnake and the Eastern Milk Snake extends from northeastern North Carolina through much of eastern Virginia, but the two apparently occur sympatrically and without interbreeding in southwestern North Carolina.

610 to 1,143 mm (24 to 45 in.) The Eastern Milk Snake has large red, brown, or gray body blotches, a pale Y-, U-, or V-shaped nape marking, and a black and white checkered venter. Juveniles typically have redder blotches than adults. Milk Snakes occur in western Virginia and the mountains of the Carolinas up to about 1,500 m elevation. They prefer woodlands but also inhabit grassy balds and meadows. Much time is spent under cover, but individuals may be active on the surface both day and night. Milk Snakes sometimes enter rural buildings, even inhabited ones. From 5 to 16 often-adherent eggs are laid in sawdust or in loose soil under objects; hatchlings average about 200 mm long.

356 to 686 mm (14 to 27 in.) The beautiful Scarlet Kingsnake has a bright pattern of red, black, and yellow or white bands that usually encircle the body. It differs from the highly venomous and superficially similar Coral Snake by having a red snout and contiguous red and black bands, as opposed to a black snout and contiguous red and yellow bands. Scarlet Kingsnakes range from southern Virginia through most of the Carolinas, but records

are scarce in much of the piedmont, and only one specimen is known from the mountains (Macon County, North Carolina). These snakes are most common in pine flatwoods on the Carolina coastal plain where they often hide under loose bark and inside logs and stumps. Scarlet King-snakes lay from three to six eggs, usually in rotten wood. Hatchlings are about 150 mm long and emerge in late summer.

Scarlet Kingsnakes and Eastern Milk Snakes are smooth-scaled constrictors, feeding chiefly on lizards, small snakes, and small mammals.

*Eastern Coachwhip (adult)*

## Eastern Coachwhip *Masticophis flagellum*

1,219 to 2,388 mm (48 to 94 in.) Probably the longest snake in the area, the slender-bodied Coachwhip is dark brown to nearly black on about the anterior third of the body, grading to pale brown or tan on the remainder. The dorsal scales are smooth. Juveniles differ from the adults by having dorsal patterns of wavy dark cross-lines which are most conspicuous anteriorly, two longitudinal rows of brown to black spots on the anterior venter, and a white outline around the large scales on top of the head. Each parietal scale has a large pale spot, and the sides of the head are prominently mottled with white.

This species ranges through most of South Carolina and in much of eastern and southern North Carolina south of Pamlico Sound. Favorite habitats are sandy flatwoods, maritime forests, and sand-hills with pines, scrub oaks, and wire grass. These snakes often occur on grassy dunes very near the ocean.

The Coachwhip's habit of frequently prowling with its head and neck raised well above the ground is unusual among local snakes. Diurnal and extremely active, it is also the most agile of our serpents. When encountered in the open, a Coachwhip crawls rapidly for the nearest hole or thick vegetation, or it sometimes climbs shrubs or small trees. However, it bites vigorously and repeatedly if cornered or restrained. This snake eats chiefly lizards, snakes,

*Eastern Coachwhip (juvenile)*

birds and their eggs, and small mammals. Even such swift lizards as Racerunners are regularly eaten, although most probably are caught by ambush or when inactive rather than by pursuit. A female Coachwhip deposits from 4 to 16 eggs per clutch in the late spring or summer. Their shells, like those of the Black Racer, bear numerous small granules resembling grains of salt. Hatchlings are about 360 mm long. Although this snake is relatively common in some parts of the Carolinas, much remains to be learned about its reproductive habits in the area.

**Green Water Snake** *Nerodia cyclopion*

762 to 1,880 mm (30 to 74 in.) This large, heavy-bodied snake is dark green, greenish brown, or brown with keeled scales. Some individuals have faint dark crossbars, but most lack distinct markings. The belly is uniformly whitish or cream colored; under the tail are pale spots on a gray or brown background. The presence of one or more small scales between the eye and the upper labials distinguishes this species from other water snakes.

Green Water Snakes prefer quiet waters of streams, lakes, ponds, and marshes. Most individuals have been captured in abandoned rice fields and rice field reservoirs. This species occurs in the southernmost quarter of South Carolina.

When caught, Green Water Snakes often bite vigorously, and adults are capable of inflicting painful but superficial scratches. Fish and frogs constitute the principal food. This species is among the most prolific snakes. The 7 to 101 young per litter are about 240 mm long at birth.

*Redbelly Water Snake (adult)*

## Redbelly Water Snake *Nerodia erythrogaster*

762 to 1,524 mm (30 to 60 in.) Adults of this large, keel-scaled water snake usually have a uniformly reddish brown to dark brown dorsum, a plain orange to reddish venter, and a white patch on the chin. Occasional specimens have white mottling and scattered dark patches on the belly. Juveniles closely resemble Northern Water Snakes by having dark brown crossbands on the neck and anterior part of the body and dorsal blotches with alternating lateral bars on the posterior part of the body. The dorsal ground color is pinkish and the venter is pale orange to pinkish, often with short brown or black bars along the edges. In contrast, Northern Water Snakes have a prominent ventral pattern of brown or reddish half-moon-shaped spots, frequently with narrow dark brown to black margins.

The Redbelly Water Snake occurs on the Delmarva Peninsula, and in the coastal plain and along the fall line from southeastern Virginia throughout the Carolinas. A fingerlike projection of the range into northwestern South Carolina to Greenville County may well have resulted from the formation of suitable habitats by recent impoundments along rivers. Favorite habitats include river swamps, marshes, lakes, and other bodies of usually still or sluggish water, but these snakes sometimes move considerable distances from aquatic environments, especially during humid

*Redbelly Water Snake (juvenile)*

periods. Individuals away from water are most often found under various kinds of surface cover around old sawdust piles and ramshackle buildings.

Like most members of the genus *Nerodia*, Redbelly Water Snakes vigorously defend themselves by biting and discharging a foul-smelling musk. Fish, toads, and frogs constitute the principal foods. Mating generally takes place in the spring and from 5 to 27 young per litter, averaging about 250 mm in total length, are born in the summer or early fall.

**Banded Water Snake** *Nerodia fasciata*

610 to 1,397 mm (24 to 55 in.) This extremely variable species differs from the closely related Northern Water Snake by having black, brown, or reddish crossbands usually throughout the length of the body, a dark stripe from the eye to the angle of the jaw, and squarish or triangular dark markings on the venter. Juveniles have bold patterns, whereas large adults often have obscure ones. The dorsal scales are strongly keeled.

These snakes are common in most permanent and semipermanent fresh water environments in the coastal plain of the Carolinas south of Albemarle Sound.

The habits of this snake are similar to those of many other water snakes. Individuals flee at the slightest disturbance, but if restrained or cornered, they bite vigorously and void musk from the cloacal glands. However, their bites, like those of other local nonvenomous snakes, produce only superficial scratches. Banded Water Snakes feed chiefly on fish and amphibians. A female produces from 9 to 57 young per litter, and the juveniles are about 200 mm long at birth.

**Northern Water Snake** *Nerodia sipedon*

610 to 1,270 mm (24 to 50 in.) This extremely variable species may
be brown, tan, gray, or reddish, usually with dark crossbands on
the neck and anterior part of the body and dark dorsal blotches and
alternating lateral bars on the remainder of the body. The undersurface is yellowish with brown or reddish half-moon-shaped
spots, frequently outlined with dark brown or black. Dorsal patterns are especially prominent in juveniles but often obscure in
large adults. The dorsal scales are strongly keeled. In Virginia
and most of North Carolina, these snakes usually have dark markings that are as wide or wider than the spaces between them.
Specimens from South Carolina generally have dark markings
that are smaller than the interspaces, especially along the sides.
Individuals living in and near brackish water along the outer banks
and adjacent mainland of North Carolina are very dark dorsally,
sometimes almost black, with black half-moons over most of the
venter.

Habitats range from mountain lakes and brooks below about
1,500 m elevation to large coastal estuaries, but this species is
absent from most of southeastern North Carolina and the coastal
plain of South Carolina.

These abundant snakes often bask on logs and other debris in
the water and along its edge. They frequently also climb among
low, overhanging limbs. Like the other water snakes, these ser-

pents have bad tempers and are often rumored to be venomous. Individuals bite readily when cornered or seized. Fish and amphibians comprise the chief food.

Contrary to popular belief, water snakes are not detrimental to fish populations. Instead, they probably contribute to better fishing by feeding largely on stunted or diseased fish. Moreover, young water snakes provide excellent food for larger game fish. The 8 to 50 young per litter, born usually in late summer, are about 200 mm long at birth.

**Brown Water Snake** *Nerodia taxispilota*

813 to 1,626 mm (32 to 64 in.) These large, heavy-bodied snakes have wide, flat heads, protruding eyes, and strongly keeled dorsal scales. The dorsum is brown with squarish black blotches, one series medially and another alternating series along each side. The yellowish venter is prominently mottled with brown or black.

Brown Water Snakes range from eastern Virginia and North Carolina through much of South Carolina, and they are most abundant in the lakes and larger streams of the coastal plain.

This species is the most arboreal of our water snakes. On sunny spring days, numerous individuals bask on limbs over the water into which they drop when disturbed. Unfortunately, many are killed by fishermen who believe them to be Cottonmouths. Like most members of the genus, Brown Water Snakes bite readily and discharge musk when handled or restrained. Fish are the favorite food. This snake mates usually in the spring, often among branches overhanging the water, and from 10 to 30 young per litter are born in summer or early fall. Neonates are about 265 mm long.

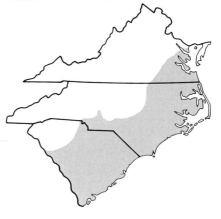

**Rough Green Snake** *Opheodrys aestivus*

559 to 914 mm (22 to 36 in.) These slender, long-tailed snakes have a uniformly green dorsum and a plain yellow or greenish yellow venter. Hatchlings and small juveniles are gray or grayish green with whitish undersurfaces. The dorsal scales are keeled.

Rough Green Snakes inhabit forested environments below about 910 m throughout most of the area. They are agile climbers but are also often seen on the ground, and many are killed on the roads. A favorite habitat is among the foliage of shrubs and small trees overhanging streams and lakes, especially in the coastal plain.

A Rough Green Snake, when first caught, may gape its mouth and expose its black interior, but it seldom attempts to bite. Spiders, grasshoppers, crickets, and insect larvae are the principal foods. A female lays from 3 to 12 eggs per clutch, usually in late spring or summer, and sometimes communal nesting occurs. One such nest in North Carolina contained 74 eggs. Hatchlings averaging about 200 mm long emerge in August or September.

**Smooth Green Snake** *Opheodrys vernalis*

356 to 610 mm (14 to 24 in.) The bright green dorsum and yellowish white venter make identification easy. This species differs from the Rough Green Snake by having smooth dorsal scales, by being smaller and stockier, and by having a more northerly range. After death, the green pigment of both species quickly fades to a pale blue. The young are grayish green above and whitish below.

Smooth Green Snakes inhabit moist, grassy meadows and fields in northwestern Virginia. A specimen, reportedly taken near the French Broad River in Madison County, North Carolina, in 1871, has been correctly identified, but the location is questionable.

Smooth Green Snakes climb in shrubs and bushes but are most often found under stones and logs. They eat insects, slugs, millipedes, centipedes, spiders, and small salamanders. A Green Snake seldom bites, even when first caught. The eggs, laid usually in June and July, vary in number from 3 to 12 per clutch. Each egg resembles a blunt-ended cylinder, and its shell is thin and parchmentlike. Hatchlings emerge by early fall and are about 130 mm long.

**Pine Snake** *Pituophis melanoleucus* (Big

1,067 to 1,829 mm (42 to 72 in.) These are large, moderately stout snakes with four prefrontals and keeled dorsal scales. Most are whitish with dark brown or black blotches that are most distinct on the posterior part of the body. In southern South Carolina, Pine Snakes frequently are tan or rusty brown, often with indistinct body blotches.

Pine Snakes occur in disjunct populations, and much remains to be learned about their distribution in the area. Sandhills with pines and scrub oaks, and sandy flatwoods are the preferred habitats in the Carolinas; in western Virginia, these snakes inhabit dry upland forests.

These handsome serpents spend much time underground and prowl on the surface chiefly in the early morning and late afternoon. They hiss loudly, vibrate the tail, and frequently bite when first caught. This powerful constrictor feeds largely on small mammals, but birds and their eggs are also eaten. Its large eggs vary in number from 3 to 12 per clutch and are laid usually in sand. Hatchlings are about 390 mm long.

**Glossy Crayfish Snake** *Regina rigida*

356 to 775 mm (14 to 30.5 in.) These small to medium-sized snakes have a shiny brown or dark olive dorsum with faint darker stripes, dark cream or orange brown lips, and a yellowish undersurface with two rows of prominent crescent-shaped black spots. The dorsal scales are keeled.

This generally uncommon species ranges in the coastal plain of the Carolinas south of Albemarle Sound, and as a disjunct population in New Kent County, Virginia. Glossy Crayfish Snakes are largely aquatic and live in marshes, cypress ponds, and sphagnum-choked canals, but individuals are seen most often at night on roads through or near these habitats.

When first handled, these snakes flatten their heads and bodies and void an especially pungent musk from the cloacal glands, and some may attempt to bite. Crayfish, dragonfly nymphs, and aquatic insect larvae constitute the bulk of the food. A North Carolina female, collected in late August, contained nine young; otherwise nothing is known about the reproductive habits of this snake.

**Queen Snake** *Regina septemvittata*

381 to 864 mm (15 to 34 in.) This slender water snake has keeled scales, a small head, and yellow lips. Its dorsum is dark brown, sometimes with three usually obscure black stripes. A yellow stripe along each lower side involves the first and second scale rows. The yellowish venter, variously striped or mottled with brown or tan, has a dark brown stripe along each side. Juveniles generally have brighter patterns than adults.

In our area, this species occurs in rocky streams and rivers in the piedmont and mountains up to about 760 m elevation. It has been recorded in the coastal plain only from the sandhills of North Carolina.

These snakes frequently bask on limbs over the water, but they are found most often beneath stones and debris along the water's edge. When first caught, a Queen Snake usually thrashes about and discharges musk but seldom attempts to bite. Crayfish are the chief food. The number of young per litter varies from 5 to 23, and neonates are about 200 mm long.

**Pine Woods Snake** *Rhadinaea flavilata*

254 to 381 mm (10 to 15 in.) These small snakes have a golden
brown or reddish brown dorsum and a glossy yellowish or whitish
venter. The top of the head is darker than the general ground color
and a brown line extends on each side of the head posterior to the
eye. The dorsal scales are smooth and iridescent.

This highly secretive species inhabits the lower coastal plain
of the area north to the outer banks in Dare County, North Carolina. The common name is appropriate, for these serpents often
occur under and inside rotten logs and stumps in pine flatwoods.
They are active on the surface chiefly at night.

The Pine Woods Snake has enlarged rear teeth in the upper jaw
and apparently secretes a weak
venom that immobilizes the small
frogs and lizards on which it feeds.
These snakes are, however, en-
tirely harmless to man and do
not bite, even when first caught.
The eggs are capsule shaped,
number from two to four per
clutch, and usually are laid in
decaying wood. Hatchlings are
about 140 mm long.

## Black Swamp Snake *Seminatrix pygaea*

254 to 483 mm (10 to 19 in.) Small size, glossy black dorsum, and red or orange undersurface with conspicuous black bars along the scale edges characterize this species. Dorsal scales are smooth, although they sometimes have thin light lines that superficially resemble keels.

This species occurs in the coastal plain of South Carolina and the lower coastal plain of North Carolina south of Albemarle Sound. Favorite habitats are cypress ponds, sphagnum-choked canals, ditches, and sluggish lowland streams with lush vegetation.

Much remains to be learned about this secretive and essentially aquatic snake in our area. Specimens have been collected among aquatic plants, in sphagnum moss, and beneath various debris along the water's edge. They sometimes occur on roads at night, especially after heavy summer rains. A Black Swamp Snake usually does not bite, even when first handled. Worms, leeches, small fish, and amphibians are the chief foods. At birth, the 2 to 14 young of each litter are about 150 mm long.

**Brown Snake** *Storeria dekayi*

229 to 457 mm (9 to 18 in.) The dorsum of this small serpent is brown, gray, or red, usually with a pale median stripe. Ordinarily, on each side of this stripe is a row of small black or dark brown spots. The spots of some individuals fuse and form short transverse bars. The venter is white to pinkish, sometimes with tiny black spots along each side. A newborn juvenile has a dark, virtually uniform dorsum and a prominent whitish neck band. Dorsal scales are keeled.

This species, widely distributed in the eastern half of the United States, ranges throughout Virginia and the Carolinas up to about 1,220 m elevation. Habitats vary from coastal flatwoods and drier pocosins to upland hardwood forests, but these snakes are most often found under paper, boards, and other debris in urban areas.

When handled, a Brown Snake does not bite but flattens its head and body and expels musk from the cloacal glands. Slugs and earthworms are the chief foods. The 3 to 27 young per litter are born usually in the summer and are about 100 mm long at birth.

**Redbelly Snake** *Storeria occipitomaculata*

165 to 305 mm (6.5 to 12 in.) This diminutive snake has keeled scales, a small but usually conspicuous white blotch on the next to the last upper labial, and three orange or yellowish nape spots, most often separate but sometimes fused. Frequently there is a light middorsal band bordered on each side by a black line, and some of the dorsal and lateral scales may have tiny white flecks. Most of the undersurface is red or orange, often with black or dark gray stippling forming a stripe along each side. The chin is whitish, heavily stippled with gray or black. Redbelly Snakes are highly variable. Some have a tan or brown dorsum, others are gray or almost black, and some individuals from the coastal plain of the Carolinas are glossy reddish or reddish orange dorsally and ventrally. Juveniles are usually darker and have brighter nape spots than adults.

Widely distributed in the eastern United States, Redbelly Snakes occur below about 1,700 m elevation throughout Virginia and the Carolinas. They apparently are most abundant in upland sections, but habitats include pine and wire grass flatwoods, sandhills, swamp margins, open deciduous forests, timbered hillsides, and wooded residential areas. Specimens are found most frequently under stones, logs, and similar sheltering objects. Like many

other secretive snakes, they are active on the surface mostly at night when individuals are sometimes found on roads.

A Redbelly Snake when first caught flattens its head and body, curls the upper lips in a sneer-like manner, and discharges musk from its cloacal glands, but it does not bite. Slugs and earthworms constitute the principal food. Matings of this ovoviviparous species have been reported in spring and fall. The 2 to 21 young per litter, born usually in summer or early fall, are about 76 mm long at birth.

## Southeastern Crowned Snake *Tantilla coronata*

203 to 305 mm (8 to 12 in.) This diminutive snake has a black or dark brown head and collar separated by a light band across the rear of the head. The rest of the dorsum is uniformly tan or reddish brown, and the translucent venter is plain white or yellow. The dorsal scales are smooth.

This species occurs throughout South Carolina and in most of North Carolina below 610 m elevation. It is known in Virginia only from a few counties in the western piedmont. Preferred habitats are pine flatwoods, maritime forests, sandhills, and wooded slopes.

These secretive snakes spend most of the day underground or beneath surface debris and prowl on the surface at night. They are found most often in the spring. The Crowned Snake has an enlarged and grooved rear tooth on each side of the upper jaw and apparently a weak venom, but it is completely harmless to man. Its food consists of centipedes, termites, and soft-bodied insects. A female deposits about three or four eggs per clutch, but measurements of hatchlings have not been reported.

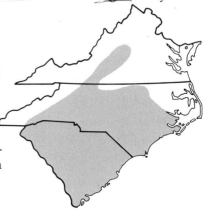

**Eastern Ribbon Snake** *Thamnophis sauritus*

457 to 965 mm (18 to 38 in.) These slender, long-tailed snakes usually have three conspicuous yellow stripes on a dark brown dorsum and a white or yellow spot in front of the eye. Along each side, one of the stripes occupies the third and fourth scale rows. Dorsal scales are keeled. Most individuals have seven upper labials per side and a prominent middorsal stripe. In extreme south-eastern South Carolina, however, many have eight upper labials per side and a less prominent or incomplete middorsal stripe.

These semiaquatic snakes occur throughout the area below about 760 m elevation. They are abundant in the coastal plain and usually rare in the mountains. Favorite habitats are marshes, damp meadows, and stream margins.

Ribbon Snakes are active and extremely agile. When alarmed, they usually disappear quickly amid vegetation. A Ribbon Snake, when seized, thrashes about but seldom bites. Amphibians and small fish are the principal food. From 3 to 20 young constitute a litter, and juveniles are about 215 mm long at birth.

### Eastern Garter Snake *Thamnophis sirtalis*

457 to 1,067 mm (18 to 42 in.) The Garter Snake is a highly variable, moderately large species with strongly keeled dorsal scales. Dorsal ground color may be various shades of green, blue, brown, or red. Often there is a conspicuous pale middorsal stripe and a less prominent light stripe involving the second and third scale rows along each side, but some individuals lack stripes and have spotted patterns.

These snakes occur throughout the area, but they are most abundant in the mountains where individuals range to or near the summits of the highest peaks. Their habitats are varied but are usually associated with moist environments, and specimens are most often found under stones and other surface cover.

A Garter Snake, when first caught, flattens its head and body, bites, and expels an especially pungent musk from its cloacal glands. Most become docile soon after capture and thrive in captivity when given proper care. Earthworms, fish, and amphibians form the bulk of the diet. The 7 to 101 young per litter are about 175 mm long at birth.

## Rough Earth Snake *Virginia striatula*

178 to 318 mm (7 to 12.5 in.) These small, secretive snakes have pointed snouts and strongly keeled dorsal scales in 17 rows around the body. The dorsum is plain brown or grayish brown, often with a pale band across the top of the head. The undersurface is glossy white or greenish white. Juveniles are usually darker and have a more prominent head band than adults.

The Rough Earth Snake occurs throughout the coastal plain and in much of the piedmont of the Carolinas. Favorite habitats range from pine and wire grass flatwoods to suburban gardens and urban lots. Sometimes many of these snakes can be found under stones, logs, and similar cover, especially in the spring.

When handled, an Earth Snake extrudes musk from its cloacal glands, but it does not bite. Earthworms are the principal food. Mating in this ovoviviparous species usually occurs in the spring, and from two to nine young are born in the summer. The young at birth are about 100 mm long.

**Smooth Earth Snake** *Virginia valeriae*

178 to 330 mm (7 to 13 in.) This small, moderately stout-bodied snake has a gray, brown, or reddish brown dorsum which may have small, scattered black spots. The venter is whitish and unmarked. The Smooth Earth Snake differs from the closely related Rough Earth Snake by having usually smooth dorsal scales in 15 rows throughout the length of the body as opposed to keeled scales in 17 rows. Smooth Earth Snakes from Highland County, Virginia, however, represent the southernmost population of a race with weakly keeled scales in 17 rows at midbody.

This species probably occurs in most of the area below about 610 m elevation, but it is generally uncommon. Records are spotty in many places and absent from western Virginia and northwestern North Carolina. These snakes are most often found beneath logs, stones, and similar surface cover in open woodlands, along forest edges, and in wooded residential areas.

This inoffensive little snake feeds chiefly on earthworms. The 2 to 14 young per litter are born in the summer and are about 90 mm long at birth.

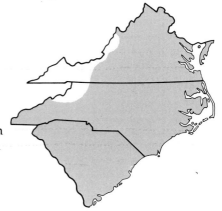

### Eastern Coral Snake *Micrurus fulvius*

508 to 890 mm (20 to 35 in.) This beautiful but highly venomous smooth-scaled snake has a black snout and colorful patterns of red, yellow, and black rings around the body. Each red and black ring is separated by a yellow ring, and the tail is banded with black and yellow.

Coral Snakes occur in the coastal plain of South Carolina and in southeastern North Carolina. Sandy flatwoods, maritime forests, and sandhills with pines, scrub oaks, and wire grass are favorite habitats.

These secretive snakes burrow in sand and ground litter and prowl on the surface chiefly in the morning and late afternoon. Their venom is extremely toxic and may produce paralysis and respiratory failure, but individuals are not aggressive and usually bite only if handled or otherwise restrained. Small lizards and snakes are the principal foods. The number of eggs per clutch varies from two to nine, and hatchlings are about 200 mm long. Much remains to be learned about this generally rare snake in our area.

*Copperhead (adult)*

2 – 4'

**Copperhead** *Agkistrodon contortrix*

610 to 1,143 mm (24 to 45 in.) Copperheads are moderately large, stout-bodied venomous snakes with a conspicuous pit on each side of the head between the eye and nostril. They have elliptical pupils that in dim light become almost round. Most subcaudal scales are undivided. Dark dumbbell- or hourglass-shaped crossbands with light centers constitute the body pattern, and the dorsal scales are keeled. Juveniles have greenish yellow tail tips. Some Copperheads in the coastal plain of the Carolinas and southeastern Virginia have a pale, often pink or tan ground color and middorsal crossbands that are very narrow (two or three scale lengths wide). In most of Virginia, and in the mountains and upper piedmont of the Carolinas, these snakes frequently have a brown or grayish brown dorsal ground color, and the middorsal crossbands are less constricted (more than three scale lengths wide).

In most of the eastern United States, the Copperhead is the most common venomous snake. It ranges throughout Virginia and the Carolinas in a variety of habitats from coastal flatwoods and drier pocosins to wooded slopes up to 910 m elevation. In some sections, it is the only venomous serpent. Individuals often hide beneath boards, pieces of tin, and similar objects around dilapidated rural buildings. Old sawdust piles are also a favorite haunt.

*Copperhead (juvenile showing yellow tail)*

Copperheads are responsible for most venomous snakebites in our area, but these snakes are not aggressive and usually bite only if stepped on or otherwise provoked. Their bites, although rarely if ever fatal to man, are serious and should receive prompt medical attention. The Copperhead eats insects, amphibians, reptiles, birds, and small mammals. Mating in this ovoviviparous species occurs most often in the spring, and a female produces from 3 to 14 young, usually in late summer. The juveniles at birth are about 215 mm long.

[242]

**Cottonmouth** *Agkistrodon piscivorus* *Large*

760 to 1,800 mm (30 to 71 in.) This highly venomous snake, often confused with several large nonvenomous water snakes, has elliptical pupils, a prominent pit on each side of the snout, and mostly undivided subcaudals on the anterior portion of the tail. Dorsal ground color is usually olive or brown, and dark crossbands with light centers constitute the body pattern. Juveniles have bright chestnut markings and yellowish tail tips, but some large adults are dark and virtually patternless. The dorsal scales are keeled.

Cottonmouths live in a variety of aquatic and semiaquatic habitats in southeastern Virginia and eastern North Carolina. They occur in much of South Carolina but are generally scarce outside the coastal plain.

When disturbed, some Cottonmouths quickly retreat; others coil, vibrate the tail, and gape the mouth widely. If further threatened, they do not hesitate to bite. This snake eats fish, amphibians, reptiles, birds, and small mammals. Its 3 to 14 young per litter average about 250 mm long and are usually born in late summer.

**Eastern Diamondback Rattlesnake** *Crotalus adamanteus*

1,067 to 1,980 mm (42 to 78 in.) This huge, heavy-bodied rattler has dark diamond-shaped body blotches with yellowish margins and light centers. A dark brown to black bar, bordered above and below by a yellow line, extends from the eye to the mouth. Dorsal ground color varies from olive to dark brown and the dorsal scales are keeled.

The Diamondback inhabits the lower coastal plain of South Carolina and the southeastern corner of North Carolina. Favorite habitats are pine flatwoods, brushy fields bordered by forests, and drier pocosins. These big rattlers frequently hide in stump holes, under brush piles, and in burrows of other animals.

The Eastern Diamondback is an impressive animal. When aroused, it quickly assumes a defensive posture: body coiled, rattle erect and buzzing, neck flexed with head directly facing the source of annoyance. It is the most dangerous snake in the Southeast. Adults eat mostly rabbits, but juveniles eat mice and other small mammals. The 7 to 18 young per litter, born usually in summer or early fall, are about 380 mm long.

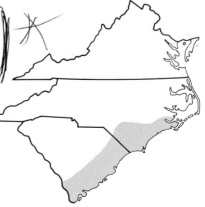

## Timber Rattlesnake *Crotalus horridus*

914 to 1,829 mm (36 to 72 in.) These are large, heavy-bodied rattle-snakes with dark blotches and wavy crossbands. Timber Rattlers from the mountains of the Carolinas and western Virginia have a yellowish or black dorsal ground color and an average of 23 rows of scales around the middle of the body. Those in southeastern Virginia and most of the Carolinas are known as Canebrake Rattle-snakes. They typically have a brown, gray, or pinkish dorsal ground color with a reddish or brown middorsal stripe, an orange to dark brown bar from the eye to the rear of the mouth, and 25 rows of scales around the middle of the body.

Timber Rattlesnakes once occurred throughout the area up to about 2,000 m elevation, but they have been eliminated from areas of extensive deforestation and human settlement. Favorite habitats are rocky hillsides, fields bordered by forests, river valleys and swamps, low pinewoods, and pocosins. In the mountains, these rattlers aggregate during the fall and spend the winter in deep crevices of rock outcrops.

Individuals often hide in stump holes and under various cover on the surface, but they may be active by day or night. Nocturnal activity is especially common during the hot summer months. When discovered, these rattlers usually remain still or attempt to escape. They are, however, extremely dangerous and vigorously defend themselves when aggravated. The presence of these and

other venomous snakes around homes and farms should be discouraged, but these animals occupy a definite place in American forests and should be left undisturbed. Small mammals, especially rodents, constitute the chief food, and if it were not for their potential danger to man and his livestock, these snakes would certainly rank high on the list of beneficial reptiles. Most matings probably take place in the spring soon after emergence from the winter dens. The young, usually born in August and September, number from 5 to 19 per litter and are about 340 mm long.

## Pigmy Rattlesnake *Sistrurus miliarius*

380 to 660 mm (15 to 26 in.) These small, moderately slender-bodied rattlesnakes have large scales on top of the head, a conspicuous pit between the eye and nostril, a slender tail, and a tiny rattle that produces a faint sound similar to the buzz of some insects. Dorsal color varies from gray to red with prominent dark brown or black blotches, and many specimens have a reddish middorsal stripe. The venter is white to pink with brown or black markings. The dorsal scales are keeled. Juveniles have a white or yellow tail tip and generally brighter patterns than adults. In extreme southeastern South Carolina, individuals are larger and darker than those from other portions of our area. Pigmy Rattlers living on and near the peninsula between Albemarle and Pamlico sounds, North Carolina, have bold glossy patterns of red, orange, or pink.

This species occurs in most of South Carolina and in southern and eastern North Carolina to Hyde County. Pine flatwoods and sandy, open woodlands with pines, wire grass, and scrub oaks are preferred habitats. In these places, Pigmy Rattlers frequently live around cypress ponds and other bodies of water. Individuals may be active on the surface both day and night, but they are often found beneath logs and other surface cover.

When disturbed, a Pigmy Rattlesnake usually attempts to crawl away, but it will strike quickly if aggravated. This species is the smallest and, along with the Copperhead, the least dangerous of our venomous snakes. Nevertheless, its bite frequently produces secondary infection and should be given prompt medical care. Frogs, lizards, and small snakes and mammals are the chief food. The 3 to 13 young per litter are about 170 mm long and are born usually in August and September.

# Glossary

**Adaptation** Any trait (anatomical, physiological, or behavioral) that makes an organism more fit to survive and reproduce in a particular habitat. Also, the process leading to the formation of such a trait.

**Adpressed Limbs** A measure of relative limb length in salamanders. A forelimb and the corresponding hind limb are laid straight against the side of the body, and the overlap of (or the distance between) their extended toes is noted. This distance is usually expressed as the number of costal folds in the region of overlap or between the tips of the limbs.

**Aestivate** To become inactive or torpid during times of drought and high temperature.

**Allopatric** Pertaining to species (or populations) that occupy nonoverlapping, but usually contiguous or adjacent, geographic ranges.

**Ambystomatids** Salamanders in the family Ambystomatidae. They inhabit North America and typically have a broad head and a stout body. Most species inhabit burrows in the soil and are rarely seen except during their short breeding season.

**Amphipods** Small crustaceans with compressed bodies. They live in and on bottom debris.

**Anastomose** To form a multibranched network.

**Arthropods** Animals with segmented bodies and appendages; the insects, crustaceans, and their relatives.

**Atrophy** To decrease in size as a result of disuse or arrested development.

**Axillary** Pertaining to the axilla, armpit.

**Barbel** Small, fleshy extension on the chin or throat as in some turtles.

**Bridge** Part of plastron which joins onto carapace in turtles.

**Bufonids** The common toads with dry warty skin and two digging tubercles on each hind foot.

**Caiman** Genus containing five species of crocodilians native to Central and tropical South America. *Caiman crocodilus*, the Spectacled Caiman, has been widely introduced into the United States.

**Carapace** The upper part of the turtle shell, including its bones and horny scutes.

**Caudal** Pertaining to the tail, situated toward the hind part of the body.

**Cenozoic Era** The last 63 million years of the earth's history; mammals, birds, and flowering plants dominate.

**Chemoreceptors** Smell and taste receptors (sensory cells or organs).

**Chironomids** Minute, delicate, mosquitolike insects. Adults are known as midges. Larvae are abundant in bottom debris and silt, and those of some species are called bloodworms.

**Cirrus** A small fingerlike projection on the upper lip of males of some plethodontid salamanders.

**Cline** A pattern of gradual change in a character from one part of the geographic range of a population to another.

**Cloaca** The chamber into which the large intestine and the urogenital ducts empty their contents.

**Communal** Pertaining to the members of a group that may cooperate in building or in using a nest but not in subsequent care of the eggs or young.

**Congeneric** Belonging to the same genus.

**Conspecific** Belonging to the same species.

**Cornification** A process wherein cells in the epidermis become thin, flat, and horny. They form scales or a thin nonliving layer which is periodically shed.

**Costal Grooves** The vertical furrows on the sides of most salamanders.

**Cranial Crest** Ridge on the head of a toad (*Bufo*).

**Cretaceous** Last geological period of the Mesozoic era, lasting about 75 million years. Dinosaurs reached their peak and became extinct.

**Crossband** A broad area of color oriented with its long axis perpendicular to the body axis.

**Crossbar** A marking (bar or stripe) that goes across rather than down the body.

**Cruciform** Cross-shaped.

**Crustaceans** A large group of the arthropods including crayfish and their relatives.

**Cryptic** Hidden, concealed, unrecognized.

**Cusp** Pointed projection on a tooth or the jaw's edge.

**Deme** A local population within which breeding is random.

**Dermis** The inner layer of the skin. It is fibrous, vascular, and sensitive.

**Devonian** A geological period of the Paleozoic era. It occurred about 370 million years ago and is referred to as the Age of Fishes.

**Digital Pad** Enlarged disklike structure at the tips of the digits of many hylid frogs.

**Dimorphism** The existence in a population of two forms or size groups and no intermediates.

**Diploid** A cell of an organism having two copies of each chromosome (one from each parent).

**Disjunct** Discontinuous, separated, not contiguous; usually refers to spatially isolated populations which formerly were parts of a large, wide-ranging population.

**Ecology** The study of the interaction of organisms with the physical environment and the other organisms which live there.

**Eft** Brightly colored, terrestrial, subadult stage of a newt.

**Electrophoretic Analysis** A laboratory technique wherein tissue extracts are subjected to an electromotive force, thus revealing (according to their relative mobilities) variant forms of proteins coded by different alleles of genes. In this way, estimates of the genetic similarity and levels of reproductive isolation among populations and species can be obtained.

**Embryology** Study of early development of organisms: their formation and growth.

**Endemic** A species or other taxon that is native to a particular place and found nowhere else.

**Eosuchia** Order of extinct, lizardlike reptiles of the Permian and Triassic; ancestors of Squamata, Rhynchocephalia, and Thecodontia.

**Epidermis** The outer layer of the skin. It is cellular and nonvascular; its outer part is cornified.

**Ethology** The study of behavioral adaptations in natural environments.

**Fall Line** Boundary between the older and harder rocks of the piedmont and the loose sediments of the coastal plain. It is marked by falls or rapids along streams flowing into the coastal plain.

**Fauna** The animals of a region.

**Flatwoods** Coastal plain habitat dominated by pine (mainly longleaf or loblolly) and wire grass. Relatively open woodlands.

**Fossorial** Adapted for digging: in salamanders and lizards, the long bodies and small limbs; in toads, the digging tubercle (spade) on each hind foot; and in snakes, the smooth scales and modified snout.

**Gene Flow** The exchange of genes between populations.

**Gene Pool** All the hereditary material in a population.

**Genetic Drift** Evolution by chance rather than by selection; the tendency within small populations for heterozygous gene pairs to become homozygous, thus reducing genetic variability.

**Gular** Relating to the throat.

**Habitat** The organisms and physical environment in a particular place.

**Haploid** Having just one copy of each chromosome, as typically occurs in sex cells.

**Hedonic** Stimulating animals to mate; erotic.

**Herpetology** The scientific study of amphibians and reptiles.

**Humeral Scutes** Anteriormost pair of scales on the plastron; each is located between the gular and a pectoral scale.

**Hybridize** To produce offspring by mating of individuals from different species.

**Hybrid Swarm** The many hybrid individuals resulting from a temporary or local breakdown of reproductive isolation between related species.

**Hylids** The common treefrogs of our area. This group also includes the cricket and chorus frogs.

**Imbricate** To overlap in a regular order.

**Keel** A prominent longitudinal ridge.

**Kilogram (kg)** Equal to 2.2 lbs.

**Kilometer (km)** Equal to 0.62 miles.

**Labial** Pertaining to the lip.

**Larva** An immature stage that differs markedly from the adult.

**Life Cycle** The entire life span of an individual from its origin to reproduction.

**Life History** The series of stages and activities through which an organism normally passes from zygote formation to death.

**Marginal Scutes** Scales located along periphery of carapace.

**Melanin** A dark brown or black pigment.

**Melanophores** Special cells with dark brown or black pigment that can be dispersed or concentrated. These large cells are usually in the dermis.

**Mental Gland** A roundish bulge or elevation on the chin of certain male salamanders. Its secretion facilitates courtship.

**Mesic** Moderately moist.

**Mesozoic Era** This important chapter in the history of the earth began 230 million years ago and lasted 165 million years; reptiles and gymnosperms dominated.

**Metamorphosis** A marked change in appearance, as when a tadpole becomes a frog. This transformation is less conspicuous in salamanders.

**Microhylids** The narrow-mouthed toads with smooth moist skin, pointed head with skin fold; small and secretive.

**Mimic** To imitate in form, color, or behavior. Usually an edible species which takes on characteristics of a species noxious to predators.

**Mollusks** Members of the phylum Mollusca, including the snails and clams.

**Molt** The casting off (shedding) of the outer layer of epidermis.

**Mutation** A new feature produced by a change in the genetic constitution of an organism, more precisely a change in a very narrow portion of the nucleic acid sequence.

**Nasolabial Groove** A tiny furrow from nostril to lip of plethodontid salamanders. It facilitates olfaction.

**Neonate** Newly hatched, newborn.

**Neoteny** Process wherein certain individuals (salamanders) become sexually mature while still in the larval stage. Under suitable environmental conditions neotenic individuals undergo metamorphosis.

**Newt** A salamander in the family Salamandridae; the adults lack conspicuous costal grooves and gills but have lungs.

**Nictitating Membrane** The third eyelid, a thin membrane that is often transparent and capable of being drawn from the inner angle over the outer surface of the eye.

**Nuchal** Related to the back of the neck.

**Nuchal Scute** The medial scale of the carapace located near the neck and anterior to the vertebrals, sometimes referred to as the cervical or precentral scute.

**Nucleolus** A roundish, dense structure in the nucleus. It is rich in ribonucleic acid (pl. nucleoli).

**Occiput** Back part of head or skull.

**Ocellus** Eyelike spot of color (pl. ocelli).

**Ontogenetic** Pertaining to the development of an organism.

**Osteoderms** Bones in dermis of reptiles.

**Ostracod** Active aquatic crustaceans, 1 or 2 mm long with a clamlike shell.

**Oviparous** Pertaining to species that lay eggs.

**Ovoviviparous** Pertaining to species that produce large, yolky eggs but do not lay them. The eggs are retained in the oviduct until they hatch.

**Paedomorphosis** The retention of embryonic or larval features by adults, an evolutionary process under genetic control.

**Paleozoic Era** An early major subdivision of geological time characterized by an abundance of macrofossils: invertebrates, fish, amphibians, clubmosses, horsetails, and ferns. It extended from 600 to 230 million years ago.

**Parotoid** Large wartlike gland near the tympanum of toads.

**Parthenogenesis** The production of an organism from an unfertilized egg; unisexual reproduction.

**Pectoral Scutes** Paired scales of plastron, located just behind the humeral scales.

**Pelagic** Living in or pertaining to the open waters of the sea.

**Pelobatids** The spadefoot toads with smooth moist skin and only one digging tubercle on hind foot; very secretive.

**Permian** Last geological period of Paleozoic era. It began 280 million years ago and lasted 50 million years. Fossil amphibians waned as reptiles rapidly became dominant.

**Phenotype** The visible traits developed under the influence of an organism's genes and its environment.

**Pheromone** A glandular secretion that evokes specific behavior in another individual after tasting or smelling the secretion.

**Phylogenetic** Pertaining to evolutionary relationships and lines of descent; the origin and evolution of higher taxa.

**Physiographic** Pertaining to physiography—the study of the earth's surface (relief).

**Physiology** The study of the functions and processes of organisms and their parts.

**Plastron** The bones and horny scutes that form the ventral part of a turtle's shell.

**Pleistocene** Glacial epoch that followed the Tertiary period and preceded the Recent epoch; it began 2 million years ago and ended about 10,000 years ago.

**Plethodontids** Salamanders in the family Plethodontidae. They lack lungs, have a unique nasolabial groove, and are common in the Western Hemisphere.

**Pleural** Referring to lungs or to chest wall.

**Pleural Scutes** Large scales of carapace, located between vertebral and marginal scutes; referred to as costals by some authors.

**Pocosin** An upland swamp in the coastal plain, especially an evergreen shrub bog.

**Population** A group of conspecific individuals occupying a particular space at the same time.

**Postocular** Located posterior to the eye.

**Prefrontal** Large, usually paired dorsal scales located on snout between frontal and internasals.

**Primitive** Referring to traits that evolved early and later gave rise to other traits; ancestral. Primitive traits are usually, but not always, less complex.

**Respire** To breath, to exchange gases (as between an organism or a cell and its environment).

**Reticulate** Having a netlike pattern.

**Rugose** Having fine wrinkles.

**Savanna** A plain with scattered trees and drought-resistant undergrowth, mostly grasses.

**Scale Rows** The longitudinal rows of scales around the bodies of lizards and snakes. They are counted just anterior to the middle of the body. In snakes, the count starts with the row adjacent to the ventrals and continues diagonally over the back to the ventrals on the opposite side.

**Scute** A large scale.

**Serrate** Notched, sawlike.

**Sibling Species** Two or more closely related species, morphologically similar but reproductively isolated.

**Smooth Scale** A scale without a longitudinal ridge (keel).

**Spartina** Widely distributed genus of grasses, common in salt marshes along the coast.

**Speciation** The process wherein a population becomes genetically diverse and new species are formed.

**Species** The basic unit of taxonomy. A population or a group of populations of closely related and similar organisms that are capable of interbreeding.

**Spermatophore** A small gelatinous mass that bears a packet of sperm; it is produced by many species of salamanders.

**Sphagnum** Large genus of mosses that grow in wet, acid areas.

**Stereotyped** Conforming to a fixed or general pattern.

**Subadult** An individual that is not yet sexually mature; e.g., a transformed amphibian.

**Subcaudal** Located on the underside of the tail.

**Subocular** Located below the eye.

**Subspecies** A race or a subdivision of a species that is geographically distinct.

**Sympatric** Referring to those populations whose geographic ranges overlap.

**Talus** Rock debris or fragments at the base of a slope or cliff.

**Taxon** Any taxonomic group, e.g., order, family (pl. taxa).

**Taxonomy** The science of naming, describing, and classifying organisms into categories: phylum, class, order, family, genus, species. It is based on established principles and procedures.

**Territoriality** Defense of an area against the entry of other members of the same species; usually involves males.

**Territory** A defended area.

**Tetrapods** Vertebrates that typically have two pairs of limbs: the amphibians, reptiles, birds, and mammals.

**Thecodontia** Order of primitive, Triassic reptiles that gave rise to dinosaurs, pterodactyls, crocodilians, and birds.

**Transform** To undergo metamorphosis, to change from larval to sub-adult stage.

**Trigonal** Triangular.

**Trill** A frog call in which the same note is rapidly repeated (8–30 times per second).

**Troglobite** An animal modified for cave or subterranean life, usually lacking pigment and eyes.

**Truncate** Lacking a point, squarish.

**Tubercle** A small knoblike projection or wart.

**Tympanum** Eardrum.

**Type Locality** The place where the type specimen was collected.

**Type Specimen** The preserved specimen that serves as the base (reference) for the name of a species.

**Vent** The cloacal aperture, the posterior body opening.

**Ventrals** Large, transverse scales of snakes, useful in locomotion.

**Vertebral Scutes** The large medial scutes of the carapace. They overlay the vertebral column.

**Vocal Sac** Inflatable, elastic pouch on or near chin of male frogs and toads. A resonating chamber.

**Wrack** Dried seaweed or other debris.

**Xeric** Arid, lacking moisture.

# Useful References

Altig, Ronald. 1970. A key to the tadpoles of the Continental United States and Canada. *Herpetologica* 26:180–207

Altig, Ronald, and P. H. Ireland. 1984. A key to salamander larvae and larviform adults of the United States and Canada. *Herpetologica* 40(2):212–18.

Behler, John L., and F. Wayne King. 1979. *The Audubon Society Field Guide to North American Reptiles and Amphibians.* Knopf, New York.

Bishop, Sherman C. 1947. *Handbook of Salamanders.* Comstock Publishing Co., Ithaca, N.Y.

Bjorndal, Karen A., ed. 1981. *Biology and Conservation of Sea Turtles.* Smithsonian Institute in cooperation with World Wildlife Fund, Inc., Washington, D.C.

Carr, Archie F. 1952. *Handbook of Turtles.* Cornell University Press, Ithaca, N.Y.

*Catalogue of American Amphibians and Reptiles.* Published by the Society for the Study of Amphibians and Reptiles, started in 1963. Write Douglas H. Taylor, *Journal of Herpetology*, Department of Zoology, Miami University, Oxford, Ohio 45056.

*Catesbiana.* Newsletter of the Virginia Herpetological Society. Write Charles M. Neal, coeditor, Radford University, Radford, Va. 24142. Similar to *NC HERPS*.

Conant, Roger. 1975. *A Field Guide to Reptiles and Amphibians of Eastern and Central North America.* Houghton Mifflin, Boston.

*Copeia.* Official publication of the American Society of Ichthyologists and Herpetologists. Founded in 1913 and published quarterly, United States National Museum, Washington, D.C. 20560.

Duellman, William E., and Linda Treub. 1987. *Biology of Amphibians.* McGraw Hill, New York.

Ernst, Carl H., and Roger W. Barbour. 1973. *Turtles of the United States.* University Press of Kentucky, Lexington.

Gans, Carl, and others, eds. 1969–88. *Biology of the Reptilia.* Vols. 1–13, Academic Press, New York. Vols. 14–15, Wiley Interscience, New York. Vol. 16, Alan R. Liss, Inc., New York. This incomparable and continuing series is only for advanced students and researchers. It contains about 8,500 pages.

Goin, Coleman J., Olive B. Goin, and George R. Zug. 1978. *Introduction to Herpetology*, 3d ed. W. H. Freeman, San Francisco.

*Herpetologica.* Journal of the Herpetologists' League. Founded in 1936 and published quarterly by the Herpetologists' League. Write Joseph C. Mitchell, Department of Biology, University of Richmond, Richmond, Va. 23173.

Huheey, James E., and Arthur Stupka. 1967. *Amphibians and Reptiles of Great Smoky Mountains National Park*. University of Tennessee Press, Knoxville.

*Journal of Herpetology*. Published quarterly by the Society for the Study of Amphibians and Reptiles (formerly the Ohio Herpetological Society, 1958–66). For membership or subscription write Douglas H. Taylor, Department of Zoology, Miami University, Oxford, Ohio 45056.

Klauber, Laurence M. 1972. *Rattlesnakes: Their Habits, Life Histories, and Influence on Mankind*. 2d ed. Vols. 1 and 2. University of California Press, Berkeley.

Linsey, Donald W., and Michael J. Clifford. 1981. *The Snakes of Virginia*. University of Virginia Press, Charlottesville.

Minton, Sherman A., Jr., and Madge R. Minton. 1969. *Venomous Reptiles*. Charles Scribner's Sons, New York.

*NC HERPS*. The North Carolina Herpetological Society Newsletter. Write to North Carolina Herpetological Society, North Carolina State Museum of Natural History, P.O. Box 27647, Raleigh, N.C. 27611. This organization is primarily for students, budding herpetologists, and hobbiests.

Oliver, James A. 1955. *The Natural History of North American Amphibians and Reptiles*. Van Nostrand, Princeton, N.J.

Palmer, William M. 1974. *Poisonous Snakes of North Carolina*. North Carolina State Museum of Natural History.

Parker, H. W., and A. Grandison. 1977. *Snakes: A Natural History*. British Museum, London.

Peters, James A. 1964. *Dictionary of Herpetology*. Hafner, New York.

Porter, Kenneth R. 1972. *Herpetology*. Saunders, Philadelphia.

Pritchard, Peter C. H. 1967. *Living Turtles of the World*. T. F. H. Publications, Jersey City.

Smith, Hobart M. 1946. *Handbook of Lizards*. Comstock Publishing Co., Ithaca, N.Y.

Smith, Hobart M. 1978. *Amphibians of North America*. Golden Press, New York. This book is a guide to field identification.

Tobey, Franklin J. 1985. *Virginia's Amphibians and Reptiles: A Distributional Survey*. Virginia Herpetological Survey. Available for a modest sum from the Survey's coordinator, Rt. 1, Box 381, Purcellville, Va. 22132.

Wright, Albert H., and Anna A. Wright. 1949. *Handbook of Frogs and Toads of the United States and Canada*. 3d ed. Comstock Publishing Co., Ithaca, N.Y.

Wright, Albert H., and Anna A. Wright. 1957. *Handbook of Snakes of the United States and Canada*. Vols. 1 and 2. Comstock Publishing Co., Ithaca, N.Y.

# Index